Cooking in
Canoe Country

Robert Black

with

Susan Peterson, Carmen Black
and Maja Black

NODIN PRESS

Most of the photos in this book were taken by Sue Peterson, but others were provided by Maja Black, Jamie Wallace, David Brislance, and John Toren.

ACKNOWLEDGMENTS

We greatly benefited from adventures and conversations with other faculty and staff at the ACM Wilderness Field Station (now the Coe Wilderness Field Station) in Ely, Minnesota, especially Bill Brooks, Jim White, Chris LaLonde, Skip Wittler, Dave Lyon, Harlo Hadow, Roger and Consie Powell, Andy McCollum, Rhawn Denniston, Craig Allin, John Benson and Karla Keyes.

Our family canoe trips have long included friends and their families whose ideas and feedback have been incorporated into this book. We are especially appreciative of the friendship and input of Bill Brooks; Skip, Michelle, and Meredith Wittler; Neil Bernstein; Chris LaLonde; Jamie Wallace and Rik Smith; Andy Bauch; and Nicole, Kolt, and Andrew Knaack.

Design: John Toren

ISBN: 978-1-935666-25-7

Library of Congress Control Number: 2011927332

Nodin Press
530 N Third Street
Suite 120
Minneapolis, MN
55401

This book is dedicated to my grandfather,
Robert W. Black, who introduced me to the wonders
of both nature and cooking.

TABLE OF CONTENTS

Introduction

Northern Ontario's Quetico Provincial Park and the Boundary Waters Canoe Area Wilderness of northeastern Minnesota together contain more than two million contiguous acres of forests, lakes, bogs, and marshes that look much as they did hundreds of years ago, when the first European fur traders arrived in the region. Most of the area was logged in the early twentieth century but the boreal vegetation has returned robustly and today the two parks comprise a wilderness area that contains no towns, resorts, or summer homes. The few roads that do thread their way to this area bring fishermen and canoeists to designated entry-points from which trips into the wilderness commence. On such trips, visitors may travel by canoe for a week or two through a landscape of pristine lakes and woods unmarred by the noise of road or air traffic, the banter of television, or other marks of civilization.

I have been making trips to the BWCAW and Quetico Park with my family and friends for more than forty years, logging countless days and nights in the area. Some of the trips were celebratory—a honeymoon, an anniversary, a graduation. Others were planned solely for the purpose of fishing, viewing wildflowers and wildlife, or taking pictures. But on most occasions our trips into the Northwoods have

had nothing more specific in mind than to reconnect with the beauty of wild places, and with one another. Along the way we've battled thick clouds of mosquitoes and days of unrelenting rain. We've also endured the occasional snowstorm, forest fire, tornado, and straight-line wind. More often we've gloried in seemingly endless stretches of calm, sunny weather, traded vocalizations with loons, owls, otters, and wolves, chased bears, and hidden from angry mother moose. We have marveled at the beauty of lichens, orchids, sunrises and sunsets, and spent entire days collecting berries.

Throughout these wilderness adventures, food has also been a major focus. Canoeing can be hard work, which makes caloric intake important. The fact that most of the food we consume must be carried on our backs across the portages that connect the lakes to one another merely adds to the challenge of devising interesting meals that can be prepared our-of-doors. In this book we hope to introduce you to menu ideas, recipes, and techniques that have worked well for us.

A Few Words About Route Planning

There are many specialized publications and websites offering up-to-date details about routes through the BWCAW and Quetico Provincial Park (see For Further Reading, page 97). But a few general remarks about routes might be in order here.

In planning a route, it's important to remember that campsites are limited. Many Quetico campsites and most BWCAW sites are marked on modern maps of the region and you should be aware of campsite locations when planning routes. Also, it's a better strategy to make camp early at a good site than to push late in the day to an isolated, favored site that may be taken. Paddling and portaging after dark is not only inconvenient but can be dangerous.

We don't worry too much about distances, but usually plan trips with "short" and "long" alternative routes. We sometimes choose to take advantage of good conditions and travel a long distance in a single day. We avoid scheduling such a day ahead of time because traveling long distances during bad weather can put canoeists at risk. We have had some successful trips of over a hundred miles just to see new country, and others in which we traveled less than fifteen miles during a week.

Traveling in Groups

When traveling in groups, "veterans" need to be attentive to problems that less seasoned members of the party are likely to experience. During the excitement that almost invariably accompanies the first day

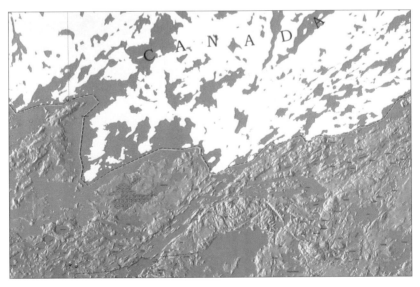

The Boundary Waters Canoe Area Wilderness and Quetico Provincial Park meet at the international border to form a labyrinth of lakes offering a wide range of travel options.

or two in the woods, it's important that everyone knows, both on portages and in camp, what's being expected of them, without dampening the enthusiasm of the group unduly. Our strategy is to not only accept the excitement (and ensuing confusion) that often accompanies the onset of a trip, but to celebrate them as a source of funny stories about being human, knowing that soon enough the bugs will get worked out and the group will settle into a solid rhythm.

I have often found that the initial excitement of wilderness travel gives way to a more mellow satisfaction once routines become established. When the members of a group are committed to a given pace and style of travel, they often develop marvelous systems for eating breakfast, breaking camp, paddling, and portaging efficiently. The joys associated with becoming efficient travelers can be intoxicating and often drives a group to extend its range on a given day. Then again, the routines that develop at a base camp around chores such as wood-gathering, water-filtering, food preparation, and clean-up can also be a source of contentment. The Northwoods never looks prettier than when you're surrounded by family or friends at a campsite with a three-day supply of seasoned, split, cedar for cooking, plenty of scrap wood for night-time campfires, ample water, a bucket of fresh-picked blueberries, and a few tasty meals ahead.

The final days of a canoe trip can be bittersweet. We've become comfortable with the rigors of paddling and portaging, the sounds of the night, the challenges of cooking over fires and balancing a plate on our lap while sitting on the ground or an old log. As our thoughts return once again to civilization, we begin to discuss how good it will be to sauna and bathe properly and to wear clean clothes again. Food also becomes a part of the conversation, as we begin to pine for the things we've been doing largely without: root beer, ice cream, fresh meat, salads, fruit pies, and Chocolate Moose cake.

Yet the range of food that can be cooked and eaten on a wilderness canoe trip is greater than many people imagine. Some canoeists like to keep things simple, getting by on little more than granola, gorp, cheese, Ry-Krisp, and the freeze-dried dinners that come in an aluminum pouch. If you fall into that category, then you will have little need for this book.

For us, the preparation of meals plays a central role. We bond together by cooking as a group and make it a point to bring food that takes time to prepare. Each meal has a chef (we rotate that role) but also many willing sous chefs who pull ingredients out of packs, cut vegetables, and cheerfully offer suggestions about the upcoming meal. This gives us more opportunities to work together and share one another's company. For us mealtime is a relaxing time for teasing, story-telling and reliving the events of each day, celebrating its wonders and consoling ourselves if we've been through a rough patch of weather or a grueling stretch of country. The comfort of hot, well-prepared food helps us recover from our losses and regroup for the next day. Beyond that, during meals we often find ourselves with plates in hand, huddled over a map spread out on the ground and anchored by cups and rocks, discussing the next day's travel options.

Clearly, food plays a significant role for us on canoe trips. That's why we pay special attention when planning trips to pack food that will make those meals memorable.

Camp Stoves and Cooking Fires

Nowadays wilderness travelers fall into two camps. Many choose to cook on stoves fueled by butane, white gas, or some other combustible material. There are several advantages to this approach. Cook stoves tend to heat things faster than wood fires, and they leave the forest surrounding a campsite untouched by wood gathering, which, even when done with the utmost care, alters the environment in subtle yet significant ways. Also, on rainy days, a cook stove will be much easier to light than a heap of soggy wood.

Yet cook stoves also have their disadvantages. You have to carry not only the stove itself, but also the fuel, which adds considerably to the load on portages and sometimes brings a noxious odor to other things in a pack. The larger the group, the more difficult it will be to prepare a satisfying meal adequately on a portable stove. Finally, those who cook on stoves tend to miss out on that "hearth-side" experience that brings a crackling, homey cheer and sense of camaraderie to the evening campsite.

Although the recipes in this book can be easily prepared on a two-burner cook stove, I myself thoroughly enjoy cooking over an open fire, and I will be referring in the text repeatedly to that heat source. But when travelling with my family or a large group, I also find it useful to pack a two-burner stove. Many of the fixed cooking-grates at BWCAW sites cannot easily be rigged with a tarp in case of rain, and we sometimes make camp too late in the day to do much wood gathering. In such cases, a two-burner camp stove can be a life-saver.

Gathering Wood and Building Fires

In the Quetico, fire rings can be makeshift; it's essential to bring your own grate.

Both Quetico Provincial Park and the Boundary Waters Canoe Area Wilderness restrict wood gathering to dead, downed wood away from the shoreline. However, newly dead (green) wood doesn't burn well and crumbling, rotting wood hardly burns at all. Campers soon learn to differentiate aromatic cedar from punky balsam, but regardless of the species, the best firewood is dry and relatively light-weight, with branches that snap off cleanly rather than bending like rubber.

We often carry large branches or small trees back to camp for processing, and may cut larger trees into lengths that can be conveniently carried to camp. When possible we *carry* wood to the campsite instead of dragging it to minimize damage to the undergrowth. It's best to restrict birch bark gathering to dead trees and stray pieces lying loose on the ground.

For managing the heat of a cooking fire, branches of wrist size or smaller often work best. They burn hot and fast and can easily be

14

A fire-tender with a good supply of small branches can keep the fire hot in just the right places, freeing the "chef" to prepare the meal.

shifted from place to place. Thicker pieces sustain a fire and establish a bed of coals. Very large pieces can be split with a hatchet or an axe, or set aside for an evening campfire.

There are nearly as many techniques for building and starting a fire as there are campers, but one method that works well for me is to place a large chunk of wood at the back of the fire pit, split side forward if possible. Pile some birchbark or other tinder next to it and then build a lean-to of small twigs over the top, allowing space between the twigs for air to circulate. When the birch bark is lit the flames will ignite the twigs above it. Be prepared with more twigs in graded sizes, adding slightly larger twigs and branches as the fire becomes established.

When preparing a meal, we often build a very vigorous fire to heat a large pot of water quickly for hot drinks and washing dishes. The resultant bed of coals can then be moved to different spots in the fire pit depending on the menu requirements. For example, when preparing a pasta meal we often boil a medium-sized pot of water for the pasta while sautéing the vegetables at another spot above the coals, focusing the flames and controlling the intensity of the fire by judiciously placing pieces of firewood onto the coals, small branches and split stems giving us the best control.

When good firewood is plentiful, we often enjoy a recreational campfire once the dishes are done. It's one of the most satisfying parts of any trip, to stare into the fire as night descends while sharing stories about the day or times long past; to drink a cup of cocoa, listen to the call of the loons, and count the stars as they appear above our heads one by one.

Every campsite in the BWCAW has a cast-iron grate like this one.

The Extravagance of Entry Day

The first day of any canoe trip is distinctive, what with the hustle and bustle of unloading gear from vehicles, packing it into canoes, and suddenly embarking on a pleasant but radically different mode of travel. It often takes a day or two for new paddlers to become comfortable with paddling and portaging, and for veteran canoeists to "shake off the rust." Some entry points are near suitable campsites, but such sites are especially popular as a result, and it isn't uncommon for a newly-entered group that had planned to stop early to find itself still on the water in the waning hours of daylight.

One thing we can count on as we make camp that first evening, however the day has gone, is an unusually rich dinner created from food items that we seldom have access to in later stages of a trip. In particular, during our first few days on the trail we often have the opportunity to make use of fresh food ingredients.

When my family and I venture out onto the lakes of the border country, our inclination is to plan a somewhat extravagant dinner on our first day to help us celebrate our return to the wilderness. If our route includes few long portages that day, we often bring along foods such as potatoes that we might otherwise consider too heavy. It's surprisingly easy to pack fragile foods such as eggs, tomatoes, and mushrooms for a few days, and to insulate foods such as meat that might otherwise spoil to keep them in perfect condition for that first dinner.

Since it's difficult to be certain just *when* we'll find a good campsite on that first day, it's important to chose a dinner menu that can be prepared quickly. All the meals I describe below can easily be prepared in sixty to ninety minutes and most can be done in far less time. (**Note: quantities here and throughout the book are for four people.**)

Taco Night

Tacos make an excellent first-night meal. They can be prepared quickly, and due to the variety of ingredients involved, everyone gets a chance to choose just what they want to eat. Our taco dinners generally include a pot of rice, instant refried beans, a meat dish, a variety of toppings, and either tortillas or hard taco shells.

Rice: We like to use white rice because of its   1 ½ C white rice
short cooking time, but brown rice or commer-
cial rice mixes also work well. We simply place the rice in a pot, cover the rice with water to a generous knuckle's height above the rice (put in more water with larger quantities of rice), then place the pot over the

fire. Bring the water to a boil, then simmer the pot gently until you observe "fish eyes"—the little volcanoes that form as the water level falls below the upper surface of the rice. At this point remove the pot from direct heat and cover it tightly with a lid or plate. We often place the rice pot on a warm rock near the fire or at the cool edge of the

fire grate. The rice will be fully cooked by the time the rest of the meal is ready. Take care not to burn the rice onto the pan as cleaning that type of mess can ruin an otherwise beautiful evening.

Instant refried beans: Add a large pot of   1 C refried bean mix
water to the fire grate while the rice is   ½ - 1 C boiling water
cooking. If the water has not been filtered,
bring it to a full boil for about five minutes, but if it has been filtered just bring it to a boil and move it to the side of the grate. You'll need a little hot water to prepare refried beans and the rest can be used for hot beverages or cleaning dinner dishes. Both red and black refried bean mixes are readily available at many grocery stores, food co-ops and outfitters. Simply add instant refried bean mix to a cup or small pot and then add enough hot water to make a thick slurry. Stir the mix well and then set the cup aside in a warm place until the mix firms up; this will only take a few minutes.

Meat: There are many ways to produce a meat dish that will make wonderful tacos. The easiest method is to brown ground beef that was packed into food packs when frozen; by evening it will be thawed but still cool to the touch. We often dice an onion

1 lb. ground beef
1 small onion
2 cloves garlic
taco seasoning/sauce
2 T cooking oil

and a few cloves of garlic and add them to the cooking meat. At this point we sometimes add dried taco seasonings or open a plastic bottle of taco sauce with which to season the cooking meat. The rice and beans will be ready by the time the meat is cooked and seasoned.

1 lb. ground beef
1 small onion
2 cloves garlic
1 t cumin
1-2 t cinnamon
½ C raisins
2 T cooking oil

ANOTHER GOOD WAY to prepare meat for tacos is to make *picadillo*. Simply brown ground beef in oil with diced onions and garlic, then add both cumin and cinnamon as the meat cooks; be sure to add enough cinnamon! Add raisins to the meat and cook gently until the raisins plump. Adjust the seasonings to taste and then you're ready to go.

It's also easy to make *chile verde* on the first night. Cube pork ahead of time, then freeze it and pack it so that it thaws during the first day of the trip. Separate the pork pieces and brown them in a little oil. Add diced onion, garlic, and green pepper to the pork and sauté for a few minutes. At this point we often add some

2 boneless pork chops
1 small onion
2 cloves garlic
1 green pepper
taco sauce
½ t cumin
½ t oregano
2 T cooking oil

Ground beef prepared with taco seasoning (left) and as picadillo (right).

liquid taco sauce and seasonings (cumin and oregano) then simmer gently until the meat is cooked.

Toppings: As the chef cooks the rice, beans, and meat, we have our sous chef prepare the taco toppings. We often carry small plastic cutting boards that fit nicely within a frying pan. The sous chef can sit with the pan in his or her lap and happily dice onions, green peppers, tomatoes, and cheese, and then keep each topping in a separate pile within the frying pan. (We found that when we used a plate to hold the toppings we often spilled diced vegetables all over the cooking area, but the sides of the frying pan contain food nicely.)

> 1 small onion
> 1 green pepper
> 1 tomato
> cheddar cheese

Steak with Garlic Mashed Potatoes

A traditional first night meal for many groups is grilled steak and mashed potatoes. Steaks should have some marbling of fat but have excess fat trimmed away prior to packing them; fat that is not eaten after the steak is cooked must be either burned or buried and can draw bears into camps. Freeze the steaks in sealed plastic bags, then insulate them and place them in the food packs frozen; the steaks will thaw during the day and be ready to be cooked in the evening. We prefer bringing fresh potatoes for this first dinner, but if the plans for entry day include many significant portages we leave the heavy potatoes behind and pack instant mashed potatoes.

> 4 small steaks
> 4 - 6 potatoes
> 1 large onion
> 2 cloves garlic
> 15 mushrooms
> 5 carrots
> margarine
> 4 T cooking oil
> steak sauce
> optional:
> 1 green pepper
> 1 zucchini
> milk/soy milk powder

Begin by removing the cooking oil, freshly thawed steak, potatoes, a few cloves of garlic, and the other ingredients from the food packs. (If you choose to bring steak sauce, be sure to transfer it to a leak-proof plastic bottle.) If our group includes individuals who are not willing or able to eat steak, we also bring additional vegetables (such as green peppers and zucchini) to fry for them with the onions and mushrooms.

If using fresh potatoes, cut large potatoes into halves or quarters, place them into a pot, cover them completely with water and place the pot directly over the cooking fire. Bring this pot to a boil,

simmer it until the potatoes are tender (15 to 20 minutes), then move the pot to the side while you cook the vegetables and steaks. (If using instant mashed potato mix, bring a pot of water to boil and keep it warm on the side of the fire until the steaks are done to your liking.)

As the potatoes cook, peel and mince the garlic, slice the onion, cut the mushrooms into slices or quarters, cut the carrots into sticks, and if you are using green peppers or zucchini cut them into small pieces or rounds. Place a frying pan or griddle over the fire and coat its surface with a thin film of cooking oil. When the oil is hot, add the onions and fry them until they begin to soften and turn translucent. If you're also cooking green peppers and zucchini, add them at this time along with the mushrooms. Sauté this mixture until the onions begin to caramelize and the other ingredients have softened, then set aside in a covered pot or plate.

Now add a thin film of oil to the frying pan or griddle and sprinkle salt and pepper on the steaks. When the oil is hot, add the steaks and cook 3-4 minutes per side, depending on the intensity of the fire and thickness of the meat. As the steaks cook, drain the potatoes and mash them with a fork or spoon. Add the minced garlic and mix it well with the potatoes. We sometimes add a little margarine or milk to enhance the smoothness of the potatoes. (If using instant mashed potatoes, follow the package instructions to prepare this dish as the steaks cook.)

Foil Dinners

Foil dinners are a favorite first night meal, and especially well-suited to any group with kids or inexperienced campfire cooks.

1 lb. ground beef
4-6 potatoes
1 onion
1-2 green peppers
2-3 tomatoes
3 carrots
spices
aluminum foil

Begin by starting a fire and feed it until a nice bed of coals has developed. Meanwhile, remove the required ingredients from the food packs. Take a square of heavy-duty aluminum foil and place a potato at the center. Meat eaters then can add a patty of seasoned ground beef on top of or next to the potato. Then add carrot sticks, onion slices, large pieces of green pepper and tomato, and sprinkle with salt, pepper, or your favorite spices (e.g. chili powder or Italian seasoning). Finally, sprinkle a few teaspoons of water on the food and fold the aluminum foil around it. We often double-wrap the food with foil as a precaution; the aluminum foil can get brittle when heated and may break open enough to let ash into the packet. Make at least one packet for each person and set them onto the coals; they should be done in 30 to 40 minutes, depending on the size of the potato and the quality of the coals. You'll need to continue adding wood from time to time to keep the coals hot, but try to avoid excessive flames directly around the packets.

If children are involved in the preparation, they'll enjoy making decisions about what size potato to use for each person and which extra

ingredients to add. We sometimes put a few extra packets containing potatoes onto the coals as we take our dinner packets off so we can have cooked potatoes for making home fries in the morning.

The downside of this meal is that you'll have to carry the used aluminum foil as garbage for the rest of the trip; it may smell strongly of meat and draw visitors you do not want.

An interesting variation of this meal is to substitute ground bison or a mixture of ground venison and pork for the ground beef.

Potatoes cook in the ashes for tomorrow's breakfast.

Curries

A lthough few people associate the Northwoods with exotic foods, many cultures feature meals that are easy to make over a cooking fire or camp stove—after all, the people who developed these dishes are, in many cases, still cooking with wood today. Curries are a prime example.

Ground lamb, rice and chapatis: This meal is best made with two or more cooks.

Begin by adding basmati or long grain rice to a pot, cover it with a generous knuckle of water, and place the pot on the fire. Adding a few pinches of turmeric will add a little flavor and considerable color to the rice, but this rice is also great on its own. As the rice boils gently, dice a small onion, the tomatoes, a few cloves of garlic and a short length of ginger root. Once the water level in the pot drops below the surface of the rice, remove the pot from direct heat and cover it tightly with a lid or plate.

1½ C rice
1 lb. ground lamb
1 small onion
2 cloves garlic
2-3 tomatoes
ginger root
2 T cooking oil
2 t curry powder
optional:
turmeric, cilantro

Now place a frying pan over the fire, add a little oil and brown the lamb. Traditional Indian cooks often heat a variety of spices, including stick cinnamon, cardamom, cloves and bay leaves, in the oil before

23

Ground lamb, rice, and chapatis.

cooking the lamb, but in the Northwoods we rely on the flavor of
the curry powder that we add as the lamb cooks. We also add diced
onion, tomatoes, garlic, and ginger, then simmer gently until all ingredients are thoroughly cooked. You might need to add a little water to
keep the mixture from drying or burning. Just prior to serving you
could add chopped cilantro as a finishing touch. Once this dish is done,
remove the pan from direct heat and cover it to keep the meat warm
while cooking the chapatis.

2 ½ C flour   *Chapati*: As one chef starts the campfire and pre-
  1 C water   pares the rice and lamb, the other should prepare
cooking oil   the dough for the chapati, a flat bread that can be
                   cooked on a griddle over a campfire. A good chapati
dough can be made by mixing flour to water in a 2½:1 ratio. Mix the
flour and water first and then knead the dough 5-10 minutes to produce
an elastic dough. Form the dough into four balls, oil them lightly and let
them rest while the other dishes are being prepared. To make the chapatis, spread flour onto a dry plate then place a ball of dough in the center
of the plate and flatten the dough. Use your hands to produce a thin
pancake about 6 inches in diameter. Sprinkle flour over the uncooked
chapatis and store them on a separate plate while you make more.

Chapatis can be cooked either in a frying pan or on a griddle.
Spread a very thin layer of oil over the surface of the pan or griddle and
place it over the fire. When the surface is hot, add as many chapatis as fit

conveniently. Cook the chapatis until they begin to brown, then turn them and brown the other side. It's often a good idea to turn them again and make sure the first side is completely done. Remove the cooked chapatis from the griddle and keep them on a warm plate while you cook the others. When all the chapatis are cooked simply add rice and the lamb mixture to a plate and eat them with the fresh-cooked chapatis.

Vegetable curry with rice: This meal also is best prepared by a team of cooks.

1½ C rice
1 onion
2 cloves garlic
4 carrots
1 small zucchini
20 green beans
1 sweet potato
2-3 potatoes
2 t curry powder
2 T cooking oil
optional: coconut

Assemble the ingredients and prepare the rice as described on page 18. As the rice cooks prepare the vegetables for cooking. Many different vegetables will work here, but we like to have fun with this dish and choose vegetables that not only taste great together but also have beautiful combinations of colors. We sometimes enhance this effect by cutting different vegetables into uniquely sized and shaped pieces. For example, we might dice an onion finely, slice carrots and summer squash into thin cross sections, cut green beans into lengths, and sweet potatoes and potatoes into medium-sized cubes.

Add a little cooking oil to a medium-sized pot, then sauté the onions until they soften. Then add the vegetables with the longest cooking times (e.g. carrots, potatoes, and sweet potatoes), cover them with water, and let them simmer gently until they become tender. At this time add the garlic, zucchini, beans, and curry powder and mix ingredients well. Adjust the liquid so nothing burns onto the pot and simmer until all the vegetables are done.

This dish can be served on either a plate or in a cup. If your curry has lots of liquid then we recommend eating it out of a cup; it can be inconvenient and sometimes disastrous to sit on the ground with a metal plate filled with hot liquid balanced in your lap! Those individuals who like flaked coconut with their curries can stir it in or sprinkle it on top at the last minute.

Stir-fries

Anyone familiar with Asian cuisine will know something of the variety of wonderful tastes that can be produced by stir-frying foods. Here are some of our favorite dishes; we're confident you'll soon discover others on your own.

Vegetables and rice: Add medium or long grain rice to a pot, then cover the rice with a generous knuckle of water. Place the pot over the fire and gently bring the rice to a boil. When the water level in the pot drops below the surface of the rice, remove the pot to the edge of the grate or a warm rock and cover the pot with a tight lid.

1½ C rice
1 small onion
2 cloves garlic
ginger root
3-4 carrots
15 mushrooms
3-4 stalks celery
1 head broccoli
1 green pepper
1 small zucchini
3 dried red peppers
2 T cooking oil
peanut butter (optional)
honey (optional)

While the rice is cooking prepare the vegetables for stir-frying. We always season stir-fried dishes with minced ginger and garlic and diced onion (dried hot peppers are optional). Some foods, such as mushrooms, celery, broccoli, red and green peppers, and summer squashes, are wonderful components of stir-fried dishes but don't store well in food packs. We often bring these vegetables for use early in the trip, keeping them in good shape for a day or two using techniques described on pages 88-89. We like to slice mushrooms length-wise, peppers into thin slivers, and broccoli stems, celery stalks, and summer squash at a slant. We cut broccoli florets into convenient pieces. We usually also slice thin cross sections of carrots, which store well in food packs, and include them in this dish.

Begin by adding oil to a frying pan or griddle that has been placed over the fire. Season the oil with slices of ginger and garlic and whole dried hot peppers. Once these items brown, remove them and commence frying the vegetables. Add the longest cooking pieces first, such as carrots and broccoli stems, and then fresh peppers and broccoli florets, to be followed by the onions, squash, and celery, and finally the mushrooms. The trick here is to have everything finish, without wilting, at the same time. We often add minced ginger and garlic to the cooking vegetables and sometimes soy sauce.

I small onion
diced ginger
2 cloves garlic
I C peanut butter
2-4 T soy sauce
water
2 T honey
I t red pepper flakes

MANY MEMBERS OF OUR extended family love to complement the flavors of stir-fries by preparing a peanut sauce (aka *gado gado*). Begin by sautéing finely diced onions, ginger and garlic in a small pot until the onion is wilted, then mix in generous amounts of peanut butter and some soy sauce. We usually thin the sauce with water at this point and often add a little honey and hot pepper flakes; mix these ingredients by stirring the sauce until it has a uniform consistency. Move the pot to the edge of the grate and simmer the sauce until it has the thickness you prefer, then remove it from the fire. Be careful not to burn the sauce onto the pot; simmer this sauce gently and stir it often.

Serve this dinner by adding the cooked rice to a plate or cup, cover the rice with fried vegetables and top it with either soy sauce or peanut sauce. Some members of our family also like to add hot sauce (which can be carried in a plastic bottle) to this dish.

Beef (or venison) and pea pods with rice: We initially made this dish with beef, but soon realized that it's also wonderful when made with venison. In either case, choose boneless cuts of meat (steaks or loin) that you then freeze and wrap so that they thaw slowly in the food pack during your first day on the water.

I ½ C rice
½ - I lb. beef
I onion
2 cloves garlic
ginger root
30-40 pea pods
cornstarch
soy sauce
2 T cooking oil

Begin by adding long grain rice to a pot, covering it with a generous knuckle of water, and simmer gently until the water level drops below the surface of the rice; then cover and move to the edge of the grate or a warm rock nearby.

While the rice is cooking, mince an inch-long piece of ginger and the garlic, dice an onion, and cut the pea pods into two or three pieces. (If small, leave them whole.) Small snap peas also work well here.

Slice the beef into thin strips no more than ¼-inch thick, an inch wide and two inches long. Place the beef strips in a small pot, then add and mix in enough cornstarch so that each strip of meat is well coated on both sides. Now add half the minced ginger and garlic and mix well. Finally, add enough soy sauce so that the meat strips become thoroughly moistened; no surfaces should be dry, but don't add so much sauce that a puddle forms in the bottom of the pot. Set the meat aside to marinate briefly while you finish preparing the vegetables.

Beef with pea pods and rice.

Now place a frying pan or griddle over the fire and add oil. When the oil is hot, add the strips of meat to the pan and fry them. Once the strips are well browned on both sides and cooked throughout, remove them to a pot or covered plate that you keep warm by the fire.

Add more oil to the frying pan or griddle and season with a few pinches of minced ginger and garlic. Add the diced onions for a few minutes, then add the pea pods. Finish this dish by adding the remaining ginger and garlic for the last minute of cooking time. At this point you can either mix the vegetables with the meat or serve each separately on top of the rice in a cup or on a plate, adding soy sauce or hot sauce if you prefer.

Note: It's easy to produce tasty variations of this dish simply by adding other vegetables, for example, red bell peppers, asparagus, or summer squash.

Spicy pork and rice: This is a wonderful first night meal. It's delicious, pleasing to the eye, and easy to make. Begin by removing the rice, pork that had been packed frozen but thawed during the day, the cooking oil, cornstarch, and other ingredients from the food packs. Add long grain rice to a pot, then cover the rice with a generous knuckle of water. Place the pot over the fire and gently bring the rice to a boil. When the water level in the pot drops below the surface of the rice, remove the pot to a warm rock and cover the pot.

1 ½ C rice
1 lb. boneless pork
1 onion
2 cloves garlic
ginger root
red pepper flakes
20 mushrooms
1 green pepper
cornstarch
soy sauce
2 T cooking oil

While the rice cooks, unwrap boneless pork cutlets or chops and slice them into thin strips about ¼-inch thick and one or two inches long. Place the pork into a small pot and coat the strips with corn-starch. Now add enough soy sauce to moisten the pork; no surfaces should be dry but don't add so much sauce that puddles form in the bottom of the pot. Let the meat stand for 10 minutes while you prepare the mushrooms and vegetables.

Slice mushrooms lengthwise, then dice a small onion and green or red bell peppers (or both). Also dice or mince a small piece of ginger and a few cloves of garlic.

Add a little cooking oil to the surface of a griddle or frying pan, brown the pork strips on both sides, then transfer the cooked meat to a pot off the fire. Now add and sauté the diced onions and peppers, the minced ginger and garlic, red pepper flakes and finally the mushrooms.

When the vegetables are done, add them to the pork, then add 1 or 2 cups of water to the combined ingredients and bring the mixture to a quick boil. We often serve this dish in cups so the extra sauce doesn't drip off hot plates onto our legs and laps; simply place rice into the bottom of the cup and cover with the meat and vegetables.

We generally use our griddle to cook batches of vegetables and then transfer them to a pot that we keep warm by the fire. We typically fry the longest cooking items first and remove them from the griddle when they're still crunchy; they'll continue to soften in the warming pot.

Sautéing onions, celery, and red peppers on the griddle.

Special Pasta Dishes

Pasta is a favorite first night dinner for many groups. The recipes below all include foods that do not store well but can be carried in food packs for at least the first day. All these dishes are easy to prepare, eye-catching, and delicious.

Fancy pasta primavera: Place a pot of water over the fire and bring it to a boil. As the water heats, remove the various ingredients from the food packs. Follow package instructions to cook the pasta.

12 oz. fettuccine
1 onion
2 cloves garlic
3-4 carrots
10 asparagus spears
20 snow peas
1 zucchini
1 red pepper
1 green pepper
Parmesan
2 T cooking oil

While the pasta cooks, prepare the various vegetables. Cut the asparagus and snow peas into one-inch lengths, zucchini and carrots into thin rounds, peppers into slivers, dice an onion and mince a few cloves of garlic. Add oil to a frying pan or griddle and when it's hot, sauté the onion. When the onion begins to wilt, add the remaining vegetables and cook for a few more minutes. Drain the cooked pasta as the vegetables finish. Add the cooked vegetables to the pasta, toss and serve on plates or in cups. (This dish is great when topped with Parmesan cheese.)

Eggplant, bell peppers, and linguine: Place a pot of water over the fire and bring it to a boil. As the water heats, remove the various ingredients from the food packs. When the water comes to a boil, cook the linguine following package instructions.

12 oz. linguine
1 onion
2 cloves garlic
1-2 eggplants
1 red pepper
1 green pepper
Parmesan
6 T cooking oil

While the pasta cooks, prepare the vegetables. Cut the eggplant into large dice, then finely dice the garlic and cut the onion and peppers into slivers. The skin of eggplants is edible but some people like to peel eggplants and then either burn the skin or pack it out. Add oil to a large frying pan or griddle and when it's hot add the eggplant. The eggplant pieces will absorb quite a bit of oil so be prepared to add more oil if necessary. Turn and cook the eggplant until it's brown on all sides; then add the onion, garlic, and peppers. When the onion is wilted and the pepper slivers have softened you're ready to eat. Drain the cooked pasta as the vegetables finish cooking.

We usually serve this dish by placing the pasta on a plate or in

Eggplant with bell peppers and linguine.

a cup, covering it with the vegetables and topping it with a generous portion of Parmesan cheese.

Bacon, mushrooms, red peppers and campanelle: Place a pot of water over the fire and bring it to a boil. While the water heats, remove the campanelle pasta, the bacon (frozen and packed so that it thaws in the food pack during the day), and the other ingredients from the food packs.

12 oz. campanelle pasta
½ - 1 lb. bacon
1 onion
20 mushrooms
1 red pepper
Parmesan
2 T cooking oil

Follow package instructions to cook the pasta. While it cooks, prepare the bacon, mushrooms, and peppers as follows.

Fry the bacon in a skillet or on a griddle until it is just done, then remove and set aside. While the bacon is cooking, slice mushrooms length-wise, cut a red pepper into slivers, and dice a small onion. Once the bacon is cooked, pour off most of the bacon fat, then fry the onion in the remaining grease. When the onion softens, add the red pepper and then the mushrooms and sauté for a few minutes.

Drain the cooked pasta, then break the bacon into pieces. Add the bacon, mushrooms, peppers, onion, and Parmesan cheese to the pasta and toss. Serve this dish on plates or in cups.

Sausage, red sauce and fettuccine: This surprising dish calls for venison or Andouille sausage, but it can also be made with summer sausage. (If you use sausage that cannot be stored at ambient temperatures, freeze and wrap the sausage so that it can thaw during your first day on the water.) We typically use tomato sauce available in plastic bottles or diced tomatoes packed in coated cardboard cartons, both of which are allowed in the Quetico and BWCAW.

12 oz. fettuccine
½ - 1 lb sausage
1 onion
2 cloves garlic
1-2 t Italian seasoning
1 carton diced tomatoes
Parmesan
2 T cooking oil

Bring a pot of water to a boil and cook fettuccine following package instructions. Slice the sausage into thin, bite-sized pieces; dice an onion and mince a few cloves of garlic.

Add a little oil to a frying pan or pot and brown the sausage pieces, then remove them and cook the onion and garlic in the same pot. At that point add the tomato sauce and return the sausage to the pot. Adjust the seasonings and heat the sauce thoroughly. Drain the cooked pasta and add it to the red sauce. Serve in cups or on plates topped with a little Parmesan cheese.

Meat or No-Meat Burgers

½ lb. ground beef
1 C falafel mix
1 onion
4 carrots
4 stalks celery
1 tomato
1 cucumber
1 T chili powder
4 buns or pitas

Most of our canoe trip groups include a few people who are dedicated meat eaters and love to pack frozen meat to be cooked the first night of the trip. Our groups also typically include a few vegetarians. It can be tricky to negotiate a first-night menu that keeps everyone happy. An easy way to do that is to bring frozen ground meat (we recommend beef or bison) to be shaped into hamburgers and also bring dried mixes for either veggie-burgers or falafel.

Begin by placing veggie-burger or falafel mix in a small pot and reconstitute it according to package instructions. (It takes a few minutes for these mixes to set up before you can shape balls of dough into patties for frying.) We make rather thin patties that fit within the palm of an adult's hand; larger patties tend to fall apart and are also more difficult to cook.

Once the patties are ready, place a frying pan or griddle over the fire and coat the surface with cooking oil. When the oil is hot add

Meat and no-meat burgers with buns and pitas.

the patties and cook for several minutes on each side. When they're done, the patties should be browned on both sides and well-cooked in the center.

While the vegetarian patties cook, make the meat patties, adding spices such as chili powder or Cajun seasoning if you wish. Keep the patties thin to insure the center gets heated through. Coat the frying pan or griddle with oil once again and then cook the meat for several minutes on each side.

Because hamburger buns are fragile and difficult to pack, we often bring pita bread or "pita-pockets," which are more durable and take up less space.

While the various burgers are cooking, we generally have the sous chef busy cutting carrots and celery stalks into thick matchsticks, and slicing onions, tomatoes, and perhaps cucumbers as toppings.

We often bring a small plastic bottle of hot mustard as condiment, and depending on the size and preferences of the group, we might also make a small pot of rice or prepare some instant refried beans.

Breakfast 2

Preparing breakfast out on the trail can be a tricky enterprise. The groups I've travelled with often have a few individuals who sleep well on the ground that first night and arise early, rested and "ready to roll" the moment they leave their tents. These high-energy types stand in marked contrast to those who don't sleep well, arise late, and emerge from their tents behaving as though they were suffering from a hangover. Grumpy people often have low tolerance for cheerful, high-energy companions, which can be problematic, especially early in the morning. We often send the early risers off to catch breakfast or on some other adventure and appoint the late risers as cooks.

The First Breakfast

This first breakfast is usually the last convenient opportunity to work with heavy, perishable, or fragile foods. For this reason we like to make it a big one, even though such meals take more time to prepare, eat, and clean-up. There are many foods that could be incorporated into a big camp breakfast, including:

Meat: For many people, few things are more appealing than the smell of cooking bacon and fresh-brewed coffee in the morning. Indeed, bacon and coffee can be mood makers for those who are not on the top of their game this first morning. A sealed package of bacon can be frozen and then insulated so that it's still safe to eat the first morning in camp. Nothing could be easier than to unwrap the package, separate the pieces, and fry them in a skillet or on a griddle. Several companies make summer sausage that can be safely stored indefinitely at ambient temperatures, and we have also packed frozen, well-insulated venison sausage which we fried up our first morning in camp. Simply unpack the sausage, slice it into thin rounds, and brown it in a frying pan or griddle.

Fish: Fishing in the Quetico and BWCAW is often so good that the early morning fishing crew is able to return to camp by 7 AM with enough fish for breakfast. In fact, we usually send a small pot and fillet knives with these fisherfolks so they can clean their fish away from camp and return with fillets (covered with water) that are ready for the frying pan.

fresh fish fillets
cornmeal
2-4 T cooking oil

Our favorite way to cook walleye, bass, and panfish for breakfast is both quick and simple. Roll each fillet in corn meal and then fry in hot oil in a frying pan or on a griddle. Brown each fillet and then flip it over to brown on the other side. Continue to cook the fillets until they're crisp on the outside surface but flake easily inside. Remove finished fish to a warm plate by the fire and cover them with another plate to keep them warm.

4-5 cooked potatoes
1 onion
2 T cooking oil
optional:
1 green pepper
1 red pepper

Potatoes: When we include potatoes in our plan for a foil dinner the first night, we often bring several additional potatoes that we wrap in aluminum foil and cook in the campfire coals before storing them overnight in a food pack. These potatoes can easily be unwrapped and sliced the next morning to make home fries or hash.

After slicing the potatoes, slice an onion. If you're interested in hash then bring along a green or red pepper and dice it coarsely. Add a little oil or bacon fat to a frying pan or griddle and fry the onions until they begin to brown.

At this point add the potato slices and brown them nicely. As the potatoes heat and brown, mix them well with the onions. Once the potatoes are ready you can serve them right away or keep them warm in a pot by the fire while you cook other items. If you choose to make hash, then dice the peppers and add them while you brown the potatoes.

Eggs: Although fresh eggs can be a mess if they break while in a food pack, it isn't difficult to bring fresh eggs on a canoe trip and keep them safe for a day or two (see pages 88-89). There are many good ways to prepare eggs over a campfire.

4-6 eggs
2 T cooking oil

One option is to heat a thin coat of oil in a frying pan or griddle and simply fry the eggs until they're done to order. Another option is to beat several eggs in a large cup or small pot and then scramble them, stirring often so they don't burn onto the pan.

4-6 eggs
I small onion
I0 asparagus spears
I5 mushrooms
I small zucchini
I tomato
2 T cooking oil

We also sometimes make a "Backwoods frittata" with fresh eggs. We dice a small onion and a tomato, then cut asparagus stalks into 1-2 inch lengths and slice mushrooms length-wise and the zucchini into rounds. Sauté the vegetables and mushrooms in a little oil in a frying pan or griddle. While the vegetables cook, beat several eggs in a cup or pan. When the vegetables are done either remove them from the pan or push them to one side, add the eggs and cook them, stirring often. Return the vegetables to the pan when the eggs are nearly done and mix ingredients well.

French Toast: French toast is easy to make and almost universally enjoyed, but it requires both fresh eggs and bread that's reasonably soft and able to absorb beaten egg. Commercially available breads tend to crush easily in food packs, and we've taken to using a homemade bread (Karla's Beer Bread) that we make prior to the trip.

6-8 slices beer bread
2-3 eggs
cinnamon
nutmeg
2 T cooking oil
maple syrup
jam

Here's how to make it:
Mix 3 cups of self rising flour and 1/3 cup sugar with one bottle of beer at room temperature (light lagers work best), then pour the mix-

The first breakfast on the trail might utilize Karla's Beer Bread to make French Toast (left) and also include fried potatoes and a frittata.

ture into a greased loaf pan. Bake this bread at 350 degrees for 45 minutes, then brush melted butter or margarine over the top of the loaf and bake 15 minutes more.

3 C self-rising flour
⅓ C sugar
1 12 oz. beer

As for the french toast itself, depending upon group size, beat a few eggs into a small pot or a small frying pan with sides high enough to retain the eggs. Stir generous amounts of ground cinnamon and nutmeg into the eggs. Now place a larger frying pan or griddle over the fire, add a little oil and heat it well. Dip slices of bread into the egg-and-spice mixture so that both sides of the bread are coated, then drop the bread slices into the pan. Cook the bread until it browns well on one side, then turn it over and brown the other side. Repeat this process until both sides are done beautifully. Remove finished pieces to a warm plate by the fire or let campers eat them as they come off the fire.

We usually bring a small plastic bottle of maple syrup and a squeeze bottle of jam as accompaniments.

Breakfasts on Typical Travel Days

Though elaborate campfire breakfasts can be memorable, on many of the trips that I've been on the group often feels an urge to be out on the water early. Portages are more likely to be uncongested early in the day, and with an early start we'll have better luck arriving at a favored campsite while it's still unoccupied. Practical matters aside, on bright crisp mornings the desire to be "out there" moving across the water can lend impetus to a quick getaway.

At such times, we make it a point to prepare and eat a simple breakfast. For such occasions we typically bring a variety of breakfast foods so that everyone can choose something they really enjoy. (In large groups, where food allergies and special needs often come into play, this can be a blessing.) We set a pot of water to heat on the fire for hot drinks and hot cereal, and remove various food options from the packs, letting each person select from the array. This method works best, of course, if we've made an effort prior to the trip to canvas our hearty voyageurs to ascertain their likely preferences and stocked up accordingly.

A hearty breakfast, hot or cold, puts everyone in a good mood.

Cold breakfasts: There are many cold breakfast options, especially for the first few days of a canoe trip. Bagels are relatively heavy and may become stale or moldy after only a few days, but they're sturdy and are not crushed easily in food packs. We often bring a variety of bagels (onion, sesame, plain) and also pack peanut butter to spread on top. Dried fruit, figs, beef jerky, and almonds can also help make a simple, cold breakfast both nutritious and satisfying.

Other popular breakfast items include leftover pancakes or corn-meal griddle cakes topped with jam. During duff (non-travel) days we often make such a large batch of pancakes that we can't eat them all, and save the uneaten ones in a plastic bag with other fragile foods in the food pack. We also sometimes bring extra pancake mix that we cook up after dinner, just so we can have pancakes and jam for lunch the next day.

Many canoeists prefer cold cereal with either reconstituted dried milk or soy milk powder. Though many commercial cereals are fragile and will quickly be reduced to crumbs in the pack, a few can be packed safely (see pages 88-89). For many campers, granola is the cold cereal of choice by a wide margin. We've tried many commercial brands over the years, purchased at grocery stores and co-ops, and have come to the conclusion that homemade granola is the best. It's surprisingly easy to make, stores well in food packs, and tastes terrific when mixed with reconstituted powdered milk or soy milk powder.

To make a large batch (about 20 cups) of granola: mix 12 cups of old fashioned rolled oats with raw sunflower seeds, whole wheat flour, wheat germ, cinnamon, chopped pecans and flaked coconut (optional). After mixing, spread these ingredients in a large (16" x 22") baking pan. Now bring honey, oil, vanilla, almond extract, cinnamon, and water to a boil. Pour wet ingredients into the dry and mix together. Bake in an oven preheated to 300 degrees for about an hour, stirring every 10-15 minutes. The granola is done when it's brown and dry. It will get crunchy as it cools and you can add raisins (up to 2 cups) after baking. (For a gluten-free version, see page 90.)

12 C rolled oats
3 C sunflower seeds
½ C whole wheat flour
1 C wheat germ
2 T cinnamon
1 C chopped pecans
3 C flaked coconut
1 C honey
1 C cooking oil
2 T vanilla
dash almond extract
2 t cinnamon
1 C water
2 C raisins

Simple Hot Breakfasts: Though elaborate breakfasts are seldom appropriate for regular "travel days," there's a lot to be said for getting something hot in your stomach on cold mornings. Instant oatmeal, which comes in convenient single-serving packets, can do the trick, especially when topped with raisins and brown sugar. (It's important to note that "big eaters" can often eat two or three packets at one sitting.) You can make the oatmeal in your cup by adding hot water, thus obviating the need to dirty another pot.

Grits are another interesting option. Made from ground corn and boiled to a creamy consistency, grits are served with a dollop of butter and eaten almost every meal in the southern U.S. However, in the North, grits are usually eaten for breakfast topped with a sprinkling of brown sugar.

Both oatmeal and grits can be cooked quickly in a small pot according to package directions. Refried beans can also hit the spot. Just think of it as *huevos rancheros* without the eggs! Bring extra hot sauce for the both the grits and beans.

Lunch 3

Lunch stops are an important part of any canoe trip. Three or four hours of paddling and portaging can be tiring, and it comes as a relief to stop on a sunny rock shelf or in the shade of a tall white pine. You can relax, put your body in different positions, eat, dangle your feet in the water, and maybe take a swim. Refueling will also increase your energy levels for the afternoon paddle that lies ahead.

It's a good idea to plan ahead each morning, making sure the lunch fixings have been consolidated and made easily accessible, preferably at the top of a single pack. This would include not only the food itself but also the requisite tools, including a cutting board, knife, cups, and spoons.

Lunch early in the trip: During the first few days of a trip, we often eat fragile, perishable foods, not only because we enjoy them, but also to guard against the monotony that might otherwise dampen our enthusiasm for lunch as the choices become more limited later on. Sandwiches are still a good choice at this early stage, though it's important to pack dense, sturdy bread that won't lose its shape in the pack. Karla's Beer Bread (see recipe on pages 36-37) is just one of many options. Cheese and summer sausage both store well in packs and can be sliced on a small cutting board and incorporated into sandwiches in seconds. Tomatoes and cucumbers also can be packed (see pages 88-89) so they survive a few days, then sliced and added to sandwiches. Our extended family members love to add hot mustard to sandwiches and we often bring a plastic bottle of mustard in our lunch pack.

Almost every group we take into canoe country includes one or a few people who love to have bagels for lunch. Bagels are heavy and may not store well in warm weather, but they can be great for lunch; we may spread peanut butter on bagel halves or make bagel sandwiches with cheese and tomato.

Pita bread and pita pockets are easy to pack safely and both store at least as well as bread and bagels. We often bring instant hummus mix in our lunch supplies and also pack an empty cup and a clean spoon. Simply pour some hummus mix into the cup and then stir in enough water to produce a thick slurry. Within a few minutes the hummus will thicken and be ready to spread onto the pita. We often add sliced tomato and cucumber to produce a delicious finished product! Pita bread also serves well as a "vessel" for sliced summer sausage, cheese, and tomato.

One of the most common lunch options on canoe trips is crackers spread with peanut butter or covered with cheese and sausage. We often bring different kinds of crackers to provide some variety to this lunch. Some crackers (e.g. Wheat Thins) are very popular but crush easily and must be packed specially to remain in tact (see pages 88-89). Other types of cracker (e.g. Ry-Krisp and Wasa) are thicker and more durable but not universally relished by campers.

An important lunch item and the most important snack food on many canoe trips is "gorp" (Good Old Raisins and Peanuts), also known as trail mix. Many commercial mixes are available and quite acceptable in a pinch, but homemade gorp invariably tastes fresher and you can vary the ingredients to personal taste. Our groups adore gorp and we often make this mix together prior to the trip, sampling and

32 oz unsalted peanuts
16 oz raisins
8 oz dried cranberries
14 oz fruit bits
6 oz pumpkin seeds
6 oz cashew pieces
12 oz M & Ms
optional:
sunflower seeds
wasabi peas
sesame sticks
coconut
currants
golden raisins
chopped apricot
cheerios

arguing about components as we proceed. For long trips and large groups we often bring two or more gallon bags of home-made gorp!

The simplest versions of gorp can be made with peanuts, raisins, and M & Ms. We have developed a more elaborate recipe, for which large quantities of unsalted, shelled peanuts form the base. We add these nuts to a large bowl, then mix in one large bag of dark raisins and a smaller bag of dried cranberries. We then stir in pumpkin seeds and cashew pieces, a few bags of dried fruit bits, and at least one bag of M&Ms. We also sometimes add wasabi peas, sesame sticks, dried coconut, and other dried fruit (e.g. currants or chopped apricots). We vary the relative proportions of these ingredients according to the desires of group members. Without additions, this recipe makes a bit more than a gallon of gorp.

Carrots are another item that can bring variety to a lunch on the trail. They store well and are good both alone and when dipped in peanut butter. We also include dried fruit and squares of semi-sweet chocolate for people who like to close their meals with a touch of sweetness. To be truly decadent spread a little raspberry jam on a chocolate square!

Lunch late in the trip

It can be challenging to produce interesting lunches throughout the length of an extended canoe trip because few lunch foods store well. One good way to vary a lunch menus is by adding things you've made the night before.

Our staple foods for lunches are sturdy crackers (e.g. Ry-Krisp or

Wasa), known to many old timers as "hardtack." These crackers store well in food packs and their coarse, earthy taste, which might be overpowering at home, tends to hit the spot in the wilderness. They make a good "transport" for hummus or peanut butter and are equally tasty topped with slices of cheese or summer sausage. We try to purchase one-pound tubes or rounds of cheese covered with wax, and small tubes (8 ounces) of summer sausage; both store well prior to opening and a large group can easily eat an entire package of each during a single lunch.

Although thinner crackers can be crushed in food packs, we often try to bring medium weight crackers such as Triscuits or Wheatsworth for group members that find hardtack intolerable. These crackers may be too fragile to receive heavy peanut butter but they can be perfect for freshly mixed hummus or with cheese and sausage.

Another way to avoid monotony at lunchtime is to serve left-over pancakes or corn griddle cakes with peanut butter or jam. They store well for a day or two in plastic bags and their sweetness brings great happiness to some campers.

Fish

Most of the groups I've traveled with in the border country have included at least a few individuals who love to fish. I've been on more than a few trips composed entirely of individuals eager to eat at least some of the fish they catch. Deciding which fish to eat, and how many, is a dicey issue which can affect both the health of those involved and the viability of local fish populations.

Biologists with the Minnesota Department of Natural Resources regularly monitor the levels of toxic chemicals such as mercury and poly-chlorinated biphenyls (PCBs) in the flesh of fish from lakes and streams throughout the state. Humans who ingest high concentrations of these chemicals may suffer brain damage or a higher incidence of cancer and birth defects. Such monitoring has led the Minnesota DNR to the conclusion that fish in the BWCAW often contain low levels of mercury but rarely contain significant quantities of other toxins. The DNR also has determined that the concentration of mercury in fish varies with species, the size/age of individuals, and the watershed in which the fish lives.

Many toxins, including mercury and PCBs, have chemical properties that cause them to accumulate in the fatty tissue of fish. Lake trout and other fatty species are more likely to contain such toxins than less fatty fish. As a fish of any species ages, the toxin levels will generally increase. A good place to find more information about these issues is the Minnesota DNR website *www.dnr.state.mn.us/lakefind*, which also offers recommendations about the frequency with which fish of various species, size, and age can safely be eaten. In general, fish from the BWCAW are safe to eat, but the DNR recommends that we

do not eat the larger individuals of any species. It also recommends that women who may be pregnant limit their consumption.

Based on these recommendations, the groups I've travelled with usually resolve to eat fish as a main course no more than two or three times during a week-long trip. Over the long haul this would be considered excessive, but we're unlikely to eat fish quite so frequently at home, so our yearly fish (and mercury) consumption will still be pretty low. We try to steer clear of lake trout, and release both the smallest and largest bass, pike, and walleye, keeping the medium-sized fish for the frying pan.

Fish grow slowly in cold waters; the large bass (> 20"), pike (> 36"), or walleye (> 28") you haul in could well be more than ten years old, and maybe over twenty. The reproductive output of fish tends to increase with size, so eating the largest fish is not only potentially unhealthy but also detrimental to the fish population.

There is some evidence that heavy recreational fishing may be depleting the stocks of some game fish in certain border lakes. Some experts advocate that canoeists practice only catch-and-release fishing to counter this trend. The Minnesota DNR, however, encourages people to eat some of the fish they catch. They believe that by fine-tuning fishing regulations they can maintain healthy populations. For example, the DNR currently imposes slot limit regulations for pike on selected lakes. In these lakes, fisherfolks can legally keep small pike (usually < 24") and "trophy" pike (>36") but must return most individuals (between 24" and 36") with significant reproductive potential to the population. Our policy is to trust the fishery managers to set sound fishing regulations and to follow them.

We enjoy fishing and are committed to fishing within the regulations set by fishery managers, though on occasion we find it necessary to adjust our techniques to better comply with regulations. For example, a few years ago we were trolling lures behind the canoe as we crossed Basswood Lake, in hopes of catching some walleyes for dinner. We were using medium-sized crankbaits with multiple treble-hooks, which often work well on walleyes. On this afternoon, however, everything we caught fell into the slot-limit dimensions of medium-sized pike and needed to be returned to the lake. Unfortunately, some of the fish we reeled in had engulfed the lures so completely that removing them without damaging the fish was difficult and time consuming. We usually keep and eat all fish that might be seriously hurt by our hooks, but in this case it was against the law. We eventually switched to lures with fewer hooks and finally quit trolling altogether. The fishing was "good" but we were stopping so often to play, catch, and release big pike that our canoes were in danger of falling too far behind the rest of the group.

This very fine smallmouth bass was too big to keep.

Though trolling for fish can often be effective when crossing the lakes of the border region, portaging fish isn't easy, and we make it a point not to keep any fish until we've reached the lake where we intend to camp. We've had good luck trolling for bass, pike, and walleye along the margins of lakes with shallow or medium running minnow-like lures, and often troll for lake trout further from shore using medium or deep running lures.

We have had wonderful travel days on Basswood, Brent, Crooked, Insula, Kawnipi, Knife, Quetico, and Sturgeon Lakes that ended with perfect campsites and a stringer loaded with walleye, bass, and pike. We're always careful to only keep fish that we'll eat at dinner, but a large group of canoeists can easily consume 5 or 6 "eating-sized" walleye or bass. It's always best to clean fish away from camp and transport the fillets in plastic bags or submerged in a small pot of water.

Fish Recipes

Fried Fish and Mashed Potatoes: This meal is easy to prepare quickly and is a great way to end a day of traveling and trolling lures on a large or long lake when fishing is good. Place a large, covered pot of water on the fire and bring it to a boil quickly. As the water is heating, cut the carrots into match sticks, then pour some of the cornmeal onto a plate

fish fillets
1 - 2 C cornmeal
2 C instant mashed
   potatoes
¼ C dried milk powder
3 - 3½ C water
6 T cooking oil

or in a clean plastic bag and dip the fish fillets in the cornmeal until they're well coated. Now place a large frying pan or griddle over the fire and cover the surface liberally with oil. When the oil is hot, brown the fillets well on both sides; remove the fish when the flakes within the fillets separate easily. Keep cooked fillets warm on a covered plate by the fire while you cook the remaining fish.

Once the water boils use some in a separate pot to make instant mashed potatoes according to package directions. They should take just a few minutes to prepare.

We serve this meal by placing a large dollop of mashed potatoes on a plate and flanking it with carrot sticks and the cooked fish fillets.

fish fillets
1 onion
2 cloves garlic
4 carrots
¼ C dried vegetables
10 sun-dried tomatoes
2 bay leaves
1 t Italian or Cajun seasoning
Cheddar cheese
2 T cooking oil

Fish chowder: Begin by dicing the onions, garlic and cheese, and slice the carrots into thin rounds. Place a little oil in a medium/large pot and sauté the onions, garlic, and carrots for a few minutes. Add spices and sauté for another minute, then add water and bring the pot to a boil. As the water heats, drop in the dried vegetables and sun-dried tomatoes. Once the water boils, cover the pot and let it simmer gently until the dried vegetables and tomatoes begin to soften. At this point add the fish fillets; they will break into bite-sized pieces as they cook. Be sure to stir the chowder from time to time so food doesn't burn onto the bottom of the pot.

The chowder is ready to eat when the vegetables are cooked and the fish pieces flake apart. We serve this chowder in cups, offering hot sauce and chunks of cheese on the side.

There are many interesting ways to modify this recipe. Though

Ginger fish on a hot griddle.

potatoes are heavy, this is one recipe in which they justify the added weight in the pack. By reducing the liquid and adding rice (and perhaps a pinch of saffron) you could turn the dish into a backwoods paella. We have one dear friend who is adept at catching crayfish (by hand) to add to his paella.

Ginger fish with stir-fried vegetables: We invented this recipe during a fishing trip into the Quetico many years ago. Fishing had been very good and we had eaten fish frequently. (At that time we were unaware that due to the mercury content of the fish in this region, eating large quantities of daily could be detrimental to our health.) Some group members grew tired of a steady diet of breaded fried fish and requested that we prepare fish another way. This recipe not only satisfied their desire for a more diverse menu, but in time became our most-requested dinner.

fish fillets
1½ C rice
1 onion
4 cloves garlic
ginger root
5-6 carrots
soy sauce
6 T cooking oil
optional:
1 green pepper
1 zucchini

This recipe calls for boneless, skinless fillets, which are easy to cut away from most fish. We usually do not use pike in this recipe unless someone in the group is able to remove the plentiful y-bones from the fillets. We also rarely use this recipe with walleye fillets, which have such a wonderful, delicate flavor that we prefer to cook them in other ways that show off their unique taste and texture.

Ginger fish with stir-fried vegetables.

Begin by finely dicing the garlic and at least an inch-long piece of ginger root, then dice the onion and slice the carrots into thin rounds. Cut other vegetables into bite-sized pieces, then set all the vegetables aside.

Now cut the fish fillets into bite-sized pieces. Place the fish chunks into a small pot and cover them with soy sauce. Add half of the diced garlic and ginger to the pot and mix it well with the fish and sauce. Let the fish marinate for at least twenty minutes.

Place the long grain rice in a pot and cover it with a generous knuckle of water. Now place the pot over the fire and bring it to a boil. Boil the rice gently until the water level drops below the surface of the rice, then remove the pot from the fire and cover it. As the rice is finishing, add cooking oil to a large frying pan or griddle and heat it over the fire. When the oil begins to smoke, drop handfuls of fish pieces onto the griddle, separate them with a spatula and fry them quickly; be sure to turn the fish repeatedly to insure browning it on all sides. Don't worry if small pieces of garlic and ginger cook with the fish; this just adds flavor to the dish.

Remove the cooked fish to a plate or small pot and add more until all the fish is cooked. Then cover the fish while you stir-fry the vegetables. You might also find it necessary to post a guard to protect the fish from "tasters"; we once had a grandmother and two little girls eat most of the ginger fish we'd prepared for a group of eight while we stir-fried the vegetables!

If it isn't possible to cook the fish and vegetables together, I find it works best to stir-fry the vegetables *after* cooking the fish. It's easier to keep them crunchy that way. Add the longest-cooking vegetables (e.g. carrots) to the griddle first, then the onions and other vegetables at appropriate times, along with the remaining garlic and ginger.

We serve this dish with both soy sauce and hot sauce, and sometimes whip up some peanut sauce as well (recipe on page 27).

Lake trout and egg noodles: One of the benefits of visiting the Quetico and BWCAW in May and June is that these lakes contain healthy populations of lake trout. These delicious, cold-water-loving fish can usually be caught near the surface through-

lake trout
12 oz. egg pasta
4 T cooking oil
Parmesan

out these two months. We often troll spoons or minnow-like, diving crankbaits behind our canoes while traveling. Many large lakes (e.g. Agnes, Basswood, Brent, and Cirrus in the Quetico, and Burntside and Snowbank in the BWCAW) are well known for their lake trout fishing, but many smaller lakes (e.g. Argo, Burke, Darky, Elk, Kekakabic, and Shan Walshe lakes) also offer terrific laker fishing. Lake trout can also be caught later in the summer, but this may require using weights to bring lures into the deep, cold-water zones to which the trout have retreated.

PLACE A MEDIUM, COVERED pot of water over the fire and bring it to a boil quickly. As the water heats, remove the egg pasta, cooking oil and grated Parmesan cheese from the food packs. (Note: egg noodles are more fragile than some types of pasta and should be packed carefully.) Cut the trout into steaks 1 to 1½ inches thick. Add a little oil to a large frying pan or griddle and cook the trout steaks, turning them over after a few minutes.

Once the water boils, add the egg noodles and simmer gently, while you finish cooking the lake trout. When the pasta is done, drain it and then serve on a plate with a trout steak on the side. We often top the egg noodles with Parmesan cheese and if a lemon happens to fall out of the food packs we serve a slice with each trout steak.

Note: More fish recipes can be found on pages 64-65 and 68-69 ,in the section on later trip dinners.

5

Mid-trip Dinners on Travel Days

Dinners on travel days during the middle part of a canoe trip should be easy to prepare quickly, because there's no way to gauge how much time you'll have once you make camp or what the prospects for firewood will be. The dishes described below are both tasty and easy to prepare in an hour or less.

Pasta and Rice Dishes

We always bring several pasta dishes along on long trips. Pasta is easy to pack, easy to make quickly, and everyone seems to like it. Simply by varying the accompanying sauces and toppings we can enjoy a variety of flavors and textures, which everyone appreciates as the days of wilderness travel accumulate.

Premium macaroni and cheese: Many people are contents to purchase boxes of "mac and cheese" that are available commercially and prepare them according to package instructions. These products gener-

12 oz. elbow macaroni
8 oz. cheddar cheese
dried milk/soymilk
spices

ally produce a good meal, but we've found we can do better, and avoid leaving the cooking pot caked with dried cheese (which can be difficult to remove) by making our "mac and cheese" from scratch. This approach also gives our *voyageurs* a bit more control over the taste of their meal.

Place a covered pot of water over the fire and bring it to a boil quickly. While the water heats, remove the ingredients from the packs.

Once the water boils, add the elbow macaroni to the pot and simmer gently until the noodles are done. Meanwhile, finely dice the cheddar cheese, then set aside. When the macaroni is cooked, remove the pot from the fire and drain the pasta.

Now place a portion of the cooked macaroni into a cup and add some diced cheese, a sprinkling of dried milk, and whatever spices you prefer. As you mix the ingredients the milk powder will liquefy, the finely diced cheese will melt, and the flavors will combine nicely. This approach enables individuals to adjust their flavors as they wish, and it's much easier to wash plastic cups than a pot that might be caked with dried cheese powder.

This recipe can be enhanced by adding a soft pack of tuna or chicken to the dish. (Regulations prohibit bringing cans of tuna or chicken into the Quetico and BWCAW, but soft packs of meat are allowed.) A more elaborate dish—tuna-noodle casserole—can be created simply by adding the tuna, noodles, and cheese to a frying pan and then baking it in a reflector oven until the surface becomes crisp. The clean-up of pots with baked-on cheese can be daunting, but it's a tasty casserole.

Spaghetti with red sauce: Place a large, covered pot of water over the fire and bring it to a boil quickly. While the water heats, dice the onion and garlic.

12 oz. spaghetti
1 onion
2 cloves garlic
1 carton tomato sauce
Italian seasoning
Parmesan

Once the water boils add the spaghetti to the pot and simmer it gently until the noodles are done. While the pasta cooks, add a little oil to a smaller pot and sauté the onion and garlic until they wilt. Combine the tomato sauce or crushed tomatoes with the onion and garlic and heat it thoroughly. Adjust the seasoning of the bubbling sauce with Italian seasoning. When the spaghetti is cooked, remove the pasta pot from the fire and drain the pasta. Place a dollop of the cooked spaghetti into a cup and cover with the red sauce and a sprinkling of Parmesan cheese.

12 oz. pasta
1 onion
2 cloves garlic
4-5 carrots
spices
2 T cooking oil
Parmesan

Pasta Primavera: Place a large, covered pot of water over the fire and bring it to a boil. Once the water boils add the pasta to the pot (we like penne and spaghetti, which store well in food packs) then simmer it gently until the noodles are done. While the pasta cooks, add a little oil to a large frying pan or griddle and sauté the vegetables; add the longest cooking items (e.g. carrots) first, then add other ingredients so they're all done simultaneously. We often add spices (e.g. basil, oregano, or Italian seasoning) to the vegetables as they cook. When the pasta is cooked, remove the pot from the fire, drain the pasta, then add the vegetables and mix well. We serve this dish either on plates or in cups and often top it with grated Parmesan cheese.

Pasta Primavera.

It's a good idea to alternate rice and pasta dishes to introduce a bit of variety to the carbohydrates you consume night after night.

Lentils and rice: Begin by dicing the onion and garlic and slicing the carrots into thin rounds. Place a little oil in a medium/large pot and sauté the onions, garlic, and carrots for several minutes. Add thyme and marjoram and sauté for another minute, then add water and lentils in a 4:1 ratio and both the dried vegetables and sun-dried tomatoes. Bring the pot to a boil, then cover it and simmer gently until the lentils are done (about 45 minutes). While the lentils cook add the

1 ½ C rice
1 C green lentils
1 onion
2 cloves garlic
4 carrots,
¼ C dried vegetables
10 sun-dried tomatoes
½ t thyme
½ t marjoram
2 T cooking oil

rice to another pot and cover with a generous knuckle of water. Bring this pot to a boil, simmer it gently until the water level drops below the surface of the rice, then remove the pot from the fire and cover it with a plate or lid.

We serve this dish by adding cooked rice to a plate or cup and then spooning the lentil mixture onto it.

Chowders

Few meals can match the positive impact of hot chowder on a group of travelers at the end of a long, tiring day during wet and cold conditions. Simply holding a cup of steaming chowder with both hands not only warms them but also sets in motion a series of responses that can help recapture the day. When the soup is also nutritious and tasty, the effect of this meal on a group can be dramatic and set the stage for better days in the future. Below we describe a chowder that's delicious and easy to make quickly. Those who enjoy catching and eating fish will find another chowder recipe on page 40. 48

1 ½ C rice
1 onion
2 cloves garlic
4 carrots
½ C dried vegetables
10 sun-dried tomatoes
2 bay leaves
1 t Italian seasoning
Cheddar cheese
2 T cooking oil

Vegetable chowder with rice: Begin by dicing the onions, garlic, and cheese, and slicing the carrots into thin rounds. Place a little oil in a medium/large pot and sauté the vegetables for several minutes. Add one or two bay leaves and Italian seasoning, and sauté for another minute, then add water and bring the pot to a boil. Once the water boils, drop in the rice, dried vegetables, and sun-dried tomatoes. Cover the pot and simmer gently until the rice and vegetables are cooked and the dried tomatoes have softened; be sure to stir the chowder during cooking.

Lentils and Rice (recipe is at left).

Note: though dried vegetables make a nice contribution to this chowder, they can be expensive; also, when choosing dried vegetables, avoid mixes that have dried beans because they'll greatly increase the cooking time.

You may want to add some cheese just before serving the chowder, or offer it on the side. We also enjoy hot sauce with this meal.

Pack Presents

Many parents in the Upper Midwest are familiar with Widjiwagan, a YMCA camp located on Burntside Lake near Ely, Minnesota, on the edge of the BWCAW. My daughters Carmen and Maja have both taken Widji canoe trips and have introduced our family to some of the Widji traditions.

One that we especially enjoy is the notion of pack presents. Prior to leaving on a canoe trip, Widji campers and a counselor prepare food and equipment packs and store them overnight. During the night another counselor secretly places a few small, lightweight, inexpensive presents in the packs. When they're discovered later, they can be great morale boosters. Popular pack presents include various forms of chocolate, gummy worms, honey-roasted peanuts, pecans in a cornbread mix, candy, silly sunglasses, small flags, and collapsible kites. The mid-trip dinner bag is a good place to put them.

6

Duff Days

We often take a "duff" day (also known as a layover day or rest day) every fourth or fifth day during a long trip. Sometimes we choose to take a day off from traveling when the weather is bad, though it arguably makes more sense to travel when the weather is bad and take a duff day when it's warm and sunny. In any case, on such days some members of the party usually like to sleep late while others are out at the crack of dawn wetting their lines or cruising along the shoreline in search of moose, otters, beavers, bitterns, or loon nests. Our meal schedule on duff days typically includes a late, large breakfast or brunch and a dinner involving dishes that take a bit longer than normal to prepare. Below we describe a number of meals that have been popular with our groups.

Breakfasts

Though duff day breakfasts take more time to prepare (and clean up after) than usual, we're well into a trip before such a day arrives, which means that the most perishable and fragile foods are gone. Nevertheless, we do our best with light-weight non-perishable items augmented by foods we gather on the trail.

Pancakes: There are many commercial pancake mixes available that produce terrific pancakes over cooking fires or camp stoves. Just follow the directions on the package, making sure to stir the water or milk into the dry ingredients a little at a time so as not to inadvertently make the batter too thin. Pour the batter onto the heated griddle

3 C pancake mix
2¼ C water
6 T cooking oil
optional:
dried milk soymilk
powder
maple syrup

using a cup. Smaller pancakes are easier to flip, and are less likely to cook unevenly due to vagaries in the heat source.

The key to cooking pancakes over both a cooking fire and camp stove is control of the flame. If the fire is blazing the pancakes are likely to burn on the outside while remaining raw in the middle.

The best way to cook pancakes over a fire is to develop a good bed of coals to heat the griddle and then add small pieces of wood (e.g. thin splits of dry cedar or dry sticks as thick as your thumb) as needed to maintain a good griddle temperature. Similarly, when cooking with a camp stove, find a flame setting that keeps the griddle temperature relatively high and constant. Cook pancakes until they puff and become firm around the edges, then flip them and brown the other side. Keep finished pancakes warm on a covered plate while you cook the remaining batter or eat them hot as they come off the fire. We typically serve pancakes with maple syrup or jam, but you also can make syrup by dissolving brown sugar in hot water. Some members of our groups love to spread peanut butter on hot pancakes.

It's also easy to make your own pancake mix. We typically combine all dry ingredients in a sturdy plastic bag before the trip, then simply add oil and water to make the batter. We often bring more pancake mix than we expect to eat for breakfast so that we can have leftover cakes for snacks and lunches later. When making the batter in camp be sure to adjust the batter to a smooth consistency but avoid making

3 C all-purpose flour
6 t baking powder
3 T sugar
⅓ C dried milk or soymilk powder
4½ t egg replacer
6 T cooking oil
2 C water
maple syrup

it too thin unless you bring additional flour. Adventurous camp cooks might want to try adding the oil and water directly to the plastic bag and mix the batter in the bag; you can then pour or squeeze the batter directly from the bag to the griddle.

2½ C all-purpose flour
1½ C cornmeal
6 t baking powder
⅔ C dried milk
or soymilk powder
6 T cooking oil
4 C water
4-6 T maple syrup

Corn griddle cakes: The cuisines of many cultures include griddle cakes made either partially or entirely of corn. The recipe below results in cakes that are much like pancakes made of wheat but with added crunch and flavor.

Prior to the canoe trip, combine all dry ingredients in a plastic bag. While making the batter in camp simply add the cooking oil, water, and maple syrup to the dry ingredients. Be sure to stir the batter as you add the liquid and avoid making a batter that is too thin. This recipe is at its best when we add fresh blueberries to the batter before frying the cakes.

Cinnamon rolls: It's easy to make tasty cinnamon rolls over a fire using a reflector oven, though we find it expedient to use self-rising flour because when using yeast out-of-doors it's difficult to control the environment in which the dough rises (and we also lack the patience to wait several hours for it to do so!)

¼ C dried milk
or soymilk powder
1 C water
⅓ C sugar
⅓ C shortening
3 t egg replacer
4 C self-rising flour
4 T margarine
½ C sugar
4 t cinnamon

Begin by mixing reconstituted milk or soy milk with the sugar and shortening. Then add the egg replacer-flour mix to the liquid, a little at a time, mixing well. (We combine these two dry ingredients at home prior to the trip.) When the dough becomes easy to handle, turn it out onto a flat, lightly floured surface and roll it into a large rectangle (9 x 15 inches). You can use the griddle as the flat surface and a hard plastic water bottle as the rolling pin. Spread margarine over the surface of the dough, then sprinkle liberally with a mix of sugar and cinnamon.

Now, beginning on the long side, roll the dough tightly to form a long cylinder. Pinch the trailing edge into the roll to create a seal. Stretch the roll a bit to make it about the same diameter along the entire length of the cylinder. Cut the dough into nine cross-sections and place them slightly apart on a greased surface. At this point you're ready to bake the rolls.

Light and portable reflector ovens are available commercially and easy to fit into packs. However, we usually just pack heavy duty aluminum foil and make a simple reflector oven by folding the foil into a dome shape that's large enough to cover the pan or griddle that serves

(Top) Rolling over the dough. (Bottom) The rolls, sliced and ready to cook.

as our baking sheet. Place the oven over the coals, then slide the rolls into the oven and bake for 20 to 25 minutes. It's extremely important to control the fire during cooking and to monitor the rolls as they cook so they don't burn. It may be necessary to flip the rolls during baking so they brown evenly on both sides.

Prepare the glaze for the cinnamon rolls while they bake. Melt the margarine in a small pot, then stir in the powdered sugar and vanilla. Stir in water until the glaze has the desired consistency.

Biscuits: It's easy to make a big batch of biscuits on duff days both for brunch and to be eaten as a cold breakfast or lunch later in the trip. Biscuits made using commercial mixes are convenient and good, but it's also easy to make your own mix prior to the trip and pack it in a

3 C Bisquick
2 t dried milk/soymilk powder
1 C water
Aluminum foil

sealable plastic bag. Biscuits are at their best when eaten hot out of the reflector oven with margarine and honey or jam!

To make biscuits using a commercial mix, begin by reconstituting the dried milk powder, then combine with the Bisquick and mix well. Turn the dough out onto a rolling surface and knead it briefly. Roll the dough to a depth of ½ inch. (A hard plastic water bottle works well for a rolling pin.) Cut the dough into circles roughly 2½ inches in diameter with a top from a small peanut butter jar or simply cut interesting shapes with a knife. Put the cut dough onto an ungreased frying pan or griddle and place it over good coals inside a reflector oven made of aluminum foil. These biscuits need to bake for only 7 to 9 minutes in a 450 degree oven and often take less time in a hot reflector oven over an open fire.

Duff Day Dinners

A duff day presents the opportunity for fishing, leisurely day-trips, and casual exploring, but it also makes it easier to prepare dinners that have longer cooking times and require more careful monitoring. Here are a few of the recipes that I have found to be well worth the extra time and effort:

Bean soup: Food stores and outfitters often carry commercial mixes of dried soup beans. I have found that the more diverse mixes—some have up to fifteen types of beans!—offer more complex tastes and textures, but all the ones I've tried are good.

8 oz dried bean mix
1 onion
2 cloves garlic
4-5 carrots
10 sun-dried tomatoes
1 t cumin
1 t oregano
optional:
cheddar cheese
summer sausage

It's important to get the beans soaking early in the day. Cover them with water by several inches and check them occasionally as they expand to be sure they remain submersed. Two to three hours before dinner time, start a fire and place the pot of beans on the grill, making sure there's plenty of water in the pot. Bring the beans to a boil, cover the pot, and keep the soup at a simmer as well as you can.

Meanwhile, dice the onion and garlic, cut the carrots into bite-sized pieces, and cut the larger sun-dried tomatoes into halves or quarters. When the beans begin to simmer, stir these ingredients into the soup along with some of the spices.

Continue simmering the soup, stirring occasionally, until the beans are tender and the soup thickens. This will require fairly close monitoring. If the fire is too hot, the beans on the bottom will burn;

if it's too cold, the beans won't cook fully. It might take two hours or more to get the beans right, during which time someone will have to tend the fire, stir the soup, and monitor its progress. (We often set up a schedule of shifts to make sure the soup is brought to perfection.)

Adjust the seasonings and volume of the soup, adding water if necessary. Serve the soup in cups along with diced cheese or sausage.

Chili: This dish can be made with either red beans or pinto beans.

8 oz dried pinto beans
1 onion
2 cloves garlic
10 sun-dried tomatoes
1 T chili powder
1 t cumin
optional:
cheddar cheese
summer sausage

Begin in the morning by immersing the beans in water and letting them soak. Check the beans occasionally to be sure they remain covered.

Two to three hours before dinner time, start a fire and place the pot of beans on the grill, once again making sure there's plenty of water in the pot. Bring the beans to a boil, cover the pot, and keep the soup at a simmer as well as you can.

Meanwhile, dice the onion and garlic, and cut large sun-dried tomatoes into halves or quarters. When the beans begin to simmer, stir these ingredients into the soup along with some of the spices.

Continue simmering the soup, stirring occasionally, until the beans are tender and the chili thickens. Adjust the seasonings. If the chili is too thick, add water. If it's too thin, remove the cover for a while. Serve the chili in cups along with hot sauce or diced cheese. Another popular option is to add chopped summer sausage to the chili for the last hour or so of cooking.

Mixed rice gumbo: Blends of several types of rice, including wild, brown, and long-grained white rice, are available in many food stores.

8 oz mixed rice blend
1 onion
2 cloves garlic
5 carrots
10 sun-dried tomatoes
1 t thyme

Begin by dicing the onion and garlic, chop the carrots coarsely, and cut large sun-dried tomatoes into halves or quarters.

Add oil to a medium-large pot and sauté the onions for a few minutes, then add the garlic and carrots. When the vegetables begin to soften add the rice blend, sun-dried tomatoes, and enough water to cover the ingredients by a few inches. Cover the pot and bring it to a boil, then simmer it gently for about 45 minutes, stirring occasionally, until the rice is tender. Be sure to check the water level in the pot while it simmers and add more water if needed. Add the spices and adjust both the seasoning and the thickness of the gumbo.

We serve this gumbo in cups along with hot sauce. Boneless fish pieces, chopped summer sausage, Cajun seasoning, dried mushrooms, and dried vegetables are also fine additions.

Black beans and rice: Few meals hit the spot like a well-seasoned plate of beans and rice.

1 ½ C rice
6 oz dried black beans
1 onion
2 cloves garlic
5 sun-dried tomatoes
1 t cumin
½ t oregano

Begin shortly after breakfast by immersing the dried black beans in a few inches of water and letting them soak. Two hours before dinner, start a fire and put the pot of beans on the grill, making sure they're still well covered. Simmer the beans gently until they become tender; be sure to monitor the water level and add water if necessary to keep the beans submerged.

While the beans are cooking, dice the onion, mince the garlic, and cut the sun-dried tomatoes into halves or quarters, then stir all ingredients into the beans. When the beans become tender add the spices and stir well. Now place long grain rice in a pot and cover with a generous knuckle of water. Bring it to a boil and simmer gently until the water level falls below the surface of the rice. At that point, remove the rice from the fire and cover tightly with a lid. Let the rice sit for several minutes, adjust the seasoning of the beans, and you're ready to eat.

Fried fish with dried mushrooms and wild rice: I can imagine few meals more representative of the Northwoods than fish and wild rice. It seems fitting to serve both for dinner after paddling through the wild rice beds that can be found in shallow water in many of the lakes of the Quetico and BWCAW. Wild rice generally has a longer cooking time than white rice so we often save this meal for duff

Fish fillets
8 oz. wild rice
4 C water
1 onion
2 cloves garlic
3 oz dried mushrooms
cornmeal
4 T cooking oil

days. It can be made with any of the game- or panfish in the region but we prefer to use boneless fillets from walleye or bass.

Begin by adding the wild rice and water to a pot and placing it over the fire. When the water begins to boil, cover it and move it to a spot on the grate where it receives low heat but doesn't boil rapidly; depending on the intensity of the fire and the quality of the rice, it might take forty minutes to cook it thoroughly.

While the wild rice is cooking, drop the dried mushrooms into a small pot of water to rehydrate. Dice the onion and garlic and set them aside.

The wild rice grains will expand and soften as they cook. When you notice that the rice grains begin to swell, put a little cooking oil in a frying pan or griddle and sauté the onion and garlic until they wilt. Add the rehydrated mushrooms and cook for another few minutes, then combine these ingredients with the wild rice and mix well.

While stirring the wild rice, check the water level in the pot; there should be enough water to ensure that it doesn't burn onto the pot as it continues to expand.

Now roll the fish fillets in the cornmeal until they're well coated. Add more oil to the frying pan or griddle and place it over the fire. When the oil is hot, add the fish and cook until the underside of each fillet is brown, then turn and brown the other side. The fish is done when it's golden brown on both sides and the flakes separate easily.

Remove cooked fillets to a warm plate by the fire until all the fillets are done. Serve this meal by spooning a large helping of wild rice and mushrooms onto a plate and flanking it with the cooked fish.

It's easy to modify this recipe, depending on your food supplies at the tag-end of a trip, by dicing a few carrots and sautéing them along with the onions and mushrooms, or rehydrating sun-dried tomatoes along with the mushrooms before adding them to the wild rice.

By the same token, we sometimes vary the ingredients we use to coat the fish fillets, using flour, commercial mixes, or cracker crumbs, and adding chili powder, Cajun seasoning, or Italian seasoning to the coating.

Fried fish, red beans, and cornbread: This is one of our most requested dinners.

8 oz. dried red beans
I onion
2 cloves garlic
10 sun-dried tomatoes
2 bay leaves
I t marjoram

Begin by immersing the red beans in a pot with enough water to cover them by several inches. Let them soak for at least a few hours, checking them occasionally to be sure they remain submerged. Two to three hours before dinner time, start a fire, place the pot of beans on the grate and bring the water to a boil. Try to keep the beans at a simmer while you dice the onion and garlic and cut the larger sun-dried tomatoes into halves or quarters. Stir these ingredients into the beans along with the spices and continue simmering, stirring occasionally, until the beans are tender and their juice thickens. Adjust the seasonings and volume of the beans by either adding water (if the beans are too dry) or removing the cover to allow moisture to escape (if they're too soupy).

Fried fish, red beans, and cornbread.

1 C cornmeal
1 C flour
1 T baking powder
¼ C sugar
3 t egg replacer
──────
¼ C cooking oil
1-2 t nutmeg
1+ C water
aluminum foil

WHEN THE BEANS become tender, start mixing up the cornbread. Good commercial cornbread mixes are available, but we like to make our own (see first five ingredients at left). Add the cornbread mix to a pot and convert to a batter by adding water and oil and stirring well. Now pour the batter into an oiled frying pan and form the aluminum foil into a dome-shaped reflector oven that will cover the cornbread pan. Move the bean pot to the edge of the fire grate and place the cornbread pan and reflector oven over the coals. Cook the cornbread for 15 to 20 minutes, depending upon the oven temperature.

As the cornbread cooks, prepare the fish for frying. Add a thin layer of cooking oil to the pan/griddle and quickly roll fish fillets in the cornmeal. When the oil is hot, add the fish fillets and fry until golden brown, then flip to cook the other side. Remove each fillet when it's crisp and brown on the outside and flakes easily.

Fish fillets
cornmeal
4 T cooking oil

Hot sauce goes well with the beans and margarine and honey with the cornbread. You could add chopped summer sausage to the beans, and Cajun seasoning or chili powder to the cornmeal breading.

4 C Bisquick
8 T egg-replacer
1 - 1½ C water
1 t garlic powder
1 onion
2 cloves garlic
8 oz. summer sausage
15 sun-dried tomatoes
12 oz. cheddar cheese
1 bottle tomato sauce
1 t Italian seasoning
3 T cooking oil
Optional:
red pepper flakes

Pizza: This meal can be a great group project, with one or two people masterminding the crust while others cut toppings and make the sauce. For many years we experimented with pizza crust mixes that we prepared at home and used on the trail, but eventually concluded that commercially available biscuit mixes like Bisquick offer the best balance of ease and result over an open fire.

Begin by placing the sun-dried tomatoes in water to soften. Combine the biscuit mix, egg replacer, water, and garlic powder to make a thick, pliable biscuit dough in a pot. Add a little cooking oil to each of two frying pans (or a griddle if you have a large group) and spread the oil evenly across the bottom and sides of the pans. Now transfer the dough to the pan(s) and spread it with your fingers until it covers the bottom completely.

As the dough is being made, the sous chefs can dice the onion and garlic, then slice the summer sausage and cheese. Add oil to a small pot and sauté the onions and garlic until they soften. Pour a bottle or carton of tomato or pizza sauce into the pot, combine with the onions and garlic, and heat thoroughly. As the sauce begins to simmer, adjust both the volume (add water if it's too thick) and the seasoning.

Ladle the hot pizza sauce generously onto the uncooked dough. Now layer the cheese over the sauce and distribute sun-dried tomatoes and sausage slices here and there over the cheese. (Note: different types of cheese have distinct storage and refrigeration requirements. We often make this meal with tubes of cheddar cheese that come in a wax coating and store well in food packs.)

Create a simple reflector oven by shaping heavy-duty aluminum foil into a dome that's large enough to contain one or two frying pans. Place the dome over the fire and let it warm for a few minutes, then slide the pizza pan(s) inside the dome for 15 to 20 minutes. The key to cooking pizza over a campfire is fire control. A large, hot bed of coals is ideal and will require the addition of very little wood during the time that the pizza cooks. If you do need to add wood, avoid adding so much that the fire flares significantly and a smoky inferno engulfs the pizza. Be sure to monitor the pizza crust so that it cooks through without burning; when the crust is done the cheese will be melted and the pizza will be ready to eat.

Fresh green or red peppers make a wonderful additional topping, if we still have any left by this stage of the trip.

7

Late-trip Dinners on Travel Days

Dinner menus for the last few days of a long canoe trip can challenge our ingenuity. The range of available ingredients dwindles as fresh vegetables spoil or are consumed. (Few vegetables keep well in food packs for more than ten days.) As adjustments are made to the quantities of food prepared, day after day, in response to good fishing or sluggish appetites, we often find, on the last days of a trip, an odd assortment of uncooked rice, pasta, and dried vegetables in the bottom of the pack. None of them is enough by itself to be a meal but they could all be *part* of a meal. Further complications may arise if the group decides to extend the trip for a day or two. All these factors often require that cooks be especially creative when preparing the last few dinners. Here are a few simple recipes my family and I have come up with is such situations.

Fish, refried beans and rice: Our trolling fisherfolks are often able to catch enough walleye and bass to provide the bulk of a dinner late

1 ½ C rice
1 C refried bean mix

during a canoe trip, but this can be a difficult task on warm, calm, sunny days in August. At these times at least one of us will switch our attention to northern pike and appropriate modifications of lure choice and fishing techniques (e.g. cease trolling around weed beds, but stopping to cast lures into them) often produces enough pike for dinner.

Begin by placing a large, covered pot of water over the fire and bring it to a boil; some of this hot water will be used to make the refried beans and the rest can be used for hot drinks and washing dishes. Place the rice in a second pot, cover with a generous knuckle of water, and bring to a boil. Simmer the rice gently until the water level drops below the surface of the rice, then remove the pot from the fire and cover it with a lid. When the large pot of water boils, place the refried bean mix into a cup or small pot, add hot water, and stir well; use enough water to create a thick slurry; the beans will firm up in a few minutes.

The final step will be cooking the fish. Many people prefer fish that are coated with cornmeal, bread crumbs, or batter before being fried, but these popular methods can grow tiresome near the end of a long trip. Here we provide two options for cooking fish without a coating. The first recipe works especially well with pike as they often flake apart in a way that makes it easy to remove their pesky Y-bones. The second recipe is for those who prefer spicy foods and works best with fillets that are less that ¾- inch thick.

Poached pike with Italian seasoning: Place a large frying pan on the fire grate and add a thin layer of cooking oil. When the oil is hot, add the pike fillets and quickly sear them on both sides; while searing one side, sprinkle Italian seasoning on the other side. Once the fillets are seared on both sides and most of the oil has been absorbed, add water to the pan, cover it and move it to a cooler spot on the grate where the fish can simmer gently. As the pike cooks, monitor the water level to be sure the pan doesn't become dry and burn the fish. The fillets are done when the flakes separate easily.

fresh pike fillets
2 T cooking oil
1 t Italian seasoning

fresh fish fillets
2 T cooking oil
1 t Cajun seasoning

Blackened fish: Place a large frying pan or griddle over a hot fire. As the griddle is heating, cover the surface of each fillet either with a commercial spice mix for blackened fish or simply use Cajun seasoning. When the griddle is very hot, add a little cooking oil and immediately drop the fillets into it. The underside of the fish will sear and cook quickly; when it has done so, it will be blackened. Turn the fillet and blacken the other side. Thin fillets will be cooked thoroughly without additional treatment.

Fried fish and grits: This is a great meal for late in the trip as all the dry ingredients are lightweight and not likely to spoil.

Begin by placing a large, covered pot of water over the fire and bring it to a boil. You can use some of the hot water for making grits and the rest for hot beverages and cleaning the dinner dishes.

fresh fish fillets
1 C quick-cooking grits
4 C water
cracker crumbs
4 T cooking oil

While the water is heating, remove the crackers and quick-cooking grits from the food pack. The crackers are probably crushed by this point in the trip. If not, place some in a plastic bag and crush them to produce small crumbs. Roll the fish fillets in the cracker crumbs until they're well coated, then reserve them on a plate.

Once the water has boiled, move the pot to the side of the fire grate and keep it warm. Transfer an appropriate quantity of boiling water to a smaller pot, then add quick-cooking grits and simmer gently for a few minutes. As the grits cook, place a frying pan or griddle over the fire and add a thin layer of cooking oil. When the oil is hot add the fish fillets and fry until golden brown, then flip to cook the other side. Remove each fillet when it's crisp and brown on the outside and flakes easily inside.

It's easy to produce variations in the coating of the fried fish in this meal either by mixing spices (e.g. Cajun seasoning or Italian seasoning) or by replacing the cracker crumbs with flour, cornmeal, or a commercial mix.

Fried rice: Rice, carrots, onions, and garlic all store well and are reliable foods during the later stages of a trip; ginger root often stores well for a week or more but may not last for two weeks.

1 ½ C rice
1 onion
2 cloves garlic
6 carrots
ginger root
4 oz. walnuts
2 T cooking oil
soy sauce
optional:
hot sauce

Place the rice in a pot, cover with a generous knuckle of water and bring to a boil. Simmer the rice gently and when the water level drops below the surface of the rice, remove the pot from the fire and cover it with a lid.

As the rice cooks, dice the onion, garlic, and ginger, and slice the carrots into thin rounds or lengths. Once the rice is removed from the fire, place a large frying pan or griddle on the grate, add oil and briefly toast the walnuts, then remove them to a plate. Add a bit more oil, stir-fry the carrots for a short time, then add the onions, garlic, and ginger. At this stage we may squirt a splash of soy sauce onto the vegetables for additional flavor. When the vegetables are done, transfer the walnuts and cooked rice to the pan/griddle and combine them with the vegetables.

Late pasta primavera: This version of *pasta primavera* belies the fresh, spring-like connotations of the name, but it's a perfect choice for dinner on the tail-end of a canoe trip.

12 oz. pasta
3 oz. dried vegetables
spices
grated Parmesan cheese

    Place a medium pot of water over the fire and bring it to a boil. Once the water boils, drop in the dried vegetables and simmer gently. When the vegetables begin to soften, add the pasta and return to a simmer. When both the vegetables and pasta are done drain the pot and stir in the spices. Serve this dish on a plate or in a cup and top with Parmesan cheese.

12 oz. chiocciole pasta
3-4 cloves garlic
6 oz. walnut pieces
red pepper flakes
1 t dried parsley
2 T cooking oil
Parmesan

Chiocciole with garlic and walnuts: This is a delicious dish that can be prepared quickly and easily.

    Place a medium pot of water, covered, over the fire and bring it to a boil. As the water heats, mince the garlic and chop the walnuts coarsely. When the water boils, add the pasta and simmer gently. Place a little oil in a frying pan and briefly sauté the garlic, then add the walnuts, red pepper flakes, and parsley, and toast lightly. When the pasta is done, drain it; then toss with the garlic, walnuts, spices, and Parmesan, and serve on either a plate or in a cup.

Chiocciole with garlic and walnuts.

Curried Quinoa: Quinoa (pronounced **keen**-wa) is a grain that was important to the Incas and is becoming better known in the United States. Although it's wonderful when served alone, as it often is in South America, we enjoy multi-cultural dishes and often prepare curried quinoa.

1 C quinoa
1 onion
4 carrots
2 t curry powder
½ C cashews
2 T cooking oil

Begin by dicing the onion, slicing the carrots into thin rounds, and chopping the cashews coarsely. Add a little oil to a pot, brown the cashews slightly, and then remove them to a plate. Now sauté the onion and carrots until the onion is translucent and the carrots begin to soften. At this point, add the curry powder, quinoa, and water. Bring the pot to a boil, cover, and simmer gently for about 15 minutes, stirring occasionally. Add more water if all the initial water becomes absorbed before the grain is completely cooked.

The quinoa is done when it becomes a bit translucent and the germ ring is visible around the outside edge of the grain. Prior to serving, add the toasted cashews to the pot and mix well.

Falafel, hummus and chapatis: Falafel mix, instant hummus mix, and flour all are lightweight and store well in food packs. This makes them well-suited for inclusion on a canoe trip menu.

2½ C flour
1 C water
cooking oil

To make the chapatis, begin by combining flour and water in a pot. Knead the dough 5 to 10 minutes to produce an elastic dough. Divide the dough into four balls, oil each ball lightly and then cover them with a damp cloth for a few minutes.

To form the chapatis, spread flour onto a dry plate, place a ball of dough in the center, and flatten the dough. Use your hands to produce a thin pancake about 6 inches in diameter. Sprinkle flour over each uncooked chapati and stack them on a separate plate while you make more. Cook the chapatis on an oiled frying pan or griddle until they brown, then turn them and brown the other side. Transfer the cooked chapatis to a warm plate while you cook the others.

Now place the falafel mix in a small pot and stir in water according to package instructions. It takes a few minutes for these mixes to set up before you can shape balls of dough into patties for frying. Make rather thin patties that fit within the palm of an adult's hand, as larger patties often fall apart and are more difficult to cook. Once the patties are ready, place an oiled frying pan or griddle over the fire. When the oil is hot add the patties and cook them several minutes on each side. When done the patties should be browned on both sides but well-cooked in the center. Remove cooked patties to a warm plate and set aside.

1 C falafel mix
2 T cooking oil

To PREPARE THE HUMMUS, pour the mix into a cup and stir in enough water to make a thick slurry. Within a few minutes the hummus will be ready to eat.

½ C hummus mix

To serve this meal, place a chapati on a plate, spread it with hummus, and top with a falafel patty.

Whatever's left stew: We often make this dish on the last night of a trip or when we extend our trip an extra day or two. Start by placing a large, covered pot of water over the fire and bring it to a boil. Some of this water will be used for the stew and the rest can be used for hot drinks and washing dishes.

Fresh vegetables
dried vegetables
refried bean mix
rice
pasta
spices

As the water heats, dice any remaining fresh vegetables and cut larger sun-dried tomatoes into halves or quarters. When the water boils, transfer some to a medium-sized pot, then drop in the chopped vegetables, any left-over dried vegetables, and the rice. Simmer the stew gently until the rice and dried vegetables begin to soften before adding the pasta. Return the pot to a simmer, stir the stew regularly, and adjust both the seasoning (e.g. Cajun seasoning, Chili powder or Italian seasoning) and the volume. We sometimes add refried bean mix both to add flavor to the stew and to thicken it.

8

Beverages, Snacks, and Desserts

In the Northwoods border country, water is seemingly everywhere, and sources of pollution are nowhere to be seen. As a result, the region has some of the cleanest water on earth. Yet due to the presence of digestive tract microparasites such as *giardia*, which are found wherever beavers and other aquatic mammals live, certain precautions are well worth the effort.

Drinking Water Safety

The frequency of cases involving *giardia*, though still relatively low, has increased in both the Quetico and BWCAW during the past forty years. Administrators of both parks now recommend that campers process water from lakes and streams prior to drinking it. Some long-time visitors to the region never treat their water, and claim that such added effort is a waste of time if you choose your water sources carefully. But digestive tract microparasites can leave a lifetime legacy of fatigue and unpleasant digestive issues, including both irritable bowel syndrome and food intolerances.

There is risk involved in any enterprise, and dehydration can also be a serious health concern during wilderness travel, especially in hot weather. But personal experience has led us to the conclusion that treating water on the trail is a small price to pay for continuing good health in later life.

The first step in any routine is to draw water a hundred yards off-shore on large lakes. Collapsible buckets that fit easily down the front of a pack are all you'll need to bring a gallon back to camp. On lunch breaks, draw the water well before arriving at a chosen rock shelf or portage. Avoid stagnant water, water from streams and swamps, and water near campsites whenever possible.

A lovely scene...but not a good place to get water.

Once you've got the water, the next step is to remove any microorganisms that might be present by treating it. This can be done by boiling the water, filtering it, or adding iodine tablets.

Boiling sufficient quantities of water to meet the demands of large groups in hot weather is time-consuming, especially considering that experts recommend that you boil it for at least five minutes to insure killing all microbes. If you're using an open fire, the water might well become smoke-flavored during that time—so much so that some campers drink less because it "tastes funny."

There are many water filters available that remove microbes and small particulate matter from water. Most outfitters and outdoor supply houses offer a variety of such devices. Unfortunately, most of them are designed to meet the needs of individuals or small groups, and can be problematic when used to treat water for large groups during hot weather. Typically such devices pump water through a small filter which may clog when used to process high volumes. The task of pumping can itself become tedious.

Large, gravity-flow filters capable of processing higher volumes of water have recently become available and we've had good success using them. We simply pour a few buckets of water into the bag located above the filter and then hang the apparatus from a branch. We then run a tube from the filter into our water jug, and within thirty minutes the jug is full.

A third way to purify water is to add iodine tablets to it. It's easy, but it makes the water taste funny. Some campers drink less water than they should because of the taste. In any case, there are limits to how much iodine can be safely consumed during a summer, so individuals who take more than one canoe trip need to monitor their iodine intake carefully.

Beverages

During the ardors of a canoe trip it's important for everyone to drink enough fluids. Failure to properly manage water intake can make people sick. Fortunately, it's easy to pack an assortment of beverages and drink mixes to accommodate almost every taste. Our food packs typically include a beverage bag containing quite a few such concoctions. We stow this bag near the top of a food pack to make access easy throughout the day. To the same end, we also encourage group members to bring their own water bottles.

Hot drinks: We usually pack an array of hot drinks to accommodate the different tastes of our group members. The options include coffee, tea (both black and herbal), hot chocolate, and Tang. We always survey group members about the frequency with which they expect to consume various drinks so we can shop accordingly. Please note that the failure to bring enough caffeinated drinks for people who are addicted to caffeine can cause them to develop significant and almost debilitating headaches.

Coffee: There are many ways to prepare coffee on the trail, and opinions differ widely about which is the best. The old-timers in our crew fondly remember making camp coffee from fresh grounds in a small pot or even a #10 coffee-can used only for brewing coffee. The technique was to place appropriate quantities of coffee grounds and water in a pot and then bring the pot to a boil. The coffee was boiled gently for a few minutes, then a pinch of wood ash was added. Next, a fresh egg was broken and dropped into the pot along with the broken shell. The pot was then moved off the fire for a few minutes. As it cooled slightly, the egg would bind with the grounds, cook, and sink to the bottom of the pot. (Cold water was sometimes added.) The coffee was then declared ready to drink.

The rationale behind this technique is that the wood ash and egg shell, both of which are "basic," counter the acids in the coffee, while the egg itself clears the grounds. Eggs are at a premium on the border trail, however, and few, I suspect, make coffee this way today. And no one wants to eat the egg, though we had one dog that was delighted to take on this chore.

An even more archaic method along the same lines is "wood-batch" coffee. Having boiled the coffee and water for a minute or two and removed it from the grate, someone draws a long, medium-sized, flaming branch from the fire, and after elaborate ritualistic flourishes, jabs it down into the pot while shouting "Woodbatch!" This is supposed to settle the grounds without wasting an egg.

Pouring water through a hand-held Melitta-style filter.

More conventional techniques for brewing fresh coffee include small percolators and "French presses." Such devices make good coffee but in relatively small quantities. Cleaning the pots can be a nuisance, and they're likely to break when stored in a pack.

Perhaps the easiest way of making good coffee is to pour boiling water through a hand-held Melitta-style coffee-filter holder. The quantities of water and coffee can be modified to fit any number of coffee-drinkers, though disposing properly of the grounds and filter, day after day, can be a challenge.

In recent years, the coffee drinkers in our groups have been relatively young and not as fussy about fresh-brewed coffee. We've found it convenient on such occasions to bring instant coffee or "coffee bags" that only require hot water and have minimal clean-up.

Russian Tea:
1 cup instant tea
2 cups Tang
1 tsp. cinnamon
1 tsp. cloves
1 pkg. Wylers lemonade mix
1½ cups sugar

Tea: Prior to each canoe trip we survey the members of our group for their tea preferences and pack accordingly. Tea bags are light and don't take much space in the pack so we always bring a few extra along. Hot tea can be wonderful to drink on cold, rainy days.

Even those who don't care for tea can get excited about Russian tea, which is a mix of sweet, citric, and tannic flavors that you can blend at home and package in small bags.

Hot chocolate mix is another popular choice. Some people prefer it to coffee, and others like to *add* it to their coffee. Along the same lines, the international coffee mixes available at all supermarkets can hit the spot as the sun goes down and a chill begins to creep into the air. They come in a host of *ersatz*-flavors from cappuccinos and lattes to mochas and espressos.

Although most people are familiar with powdered orange drinks (e.g. Tang) as a cold beverage, when mixed with hot water it makes an eye-opening breakfast drink.

Cold drinks: Our primary cold beverage on the trail is water, but it's a good idea to pack additional options for those who prefer flavored drinks. Our most popular drink mix is a powdered orange drink (e.g. Tang) that serves as a juice replacement at breakfast. Other popular flavors include lemonade, pink lemonade, raspberry, strawberry, and various KoolAid flavors. If such sugary drinks are being stored in water bottles, it's important to wash them regularly.

When purchasing drink powders it may be a challenge to choose the ones with appropriate sweeteners. Some come with sugar, some are artificially sweetened, and some are unsweetened.

Some people I've travelled with have enjoyed putting tea bags or freshly brewed tea in their water bottles for use during the day.

Snacks, treats, and emergency rations

It's a good idea to bring a variety of snacks and make sure some of them are accessible throughout the day. Our staple snack is gorp (see pages 42-43). We also bring a supply of semi-sweet baking chocolate (it doesn't met as easily as milk chocolate), a bag of dried fruit, a variety of fruit leathers, and a few granola bars. The chocolate, dried fruit, and leathers store well in food packs but some granola bars will crumble unless they're packed carefully. Pieces of hard candy can provide a welcome treat during a hard paddle or after a difficult portage.

Sometimes at the end of a long travel day or when conditions are difficult, we arrive at our campsite too exhausted to begin setting up camp immediately. At such times a break is in order: we relax for a few minutes and share a nutritious snack that returns the smile to tired faces and reenergizes the group. We sometimes pull the cheese, sausage, peanut butter, instant hummus mix, and crackers out of the lunch box pack and organize a second, mini-lunch. Another tempting option is to break out the camp stove, boil a small pot of water, and add an instant soup mix.

By the same token, we sometimes use the hot water to reconstitute some instant refried beans. We then place the griddle over the burners and warm some tortillas. While the tortillas heat we dice cheese, chop sausage, and perhaps dice a small onion and tomato for toppings. We then simply spread a warm tortilla with refried beans and cover it with toppings; the heat of the tortilla and beans often melts the cheese.

Snacks of this kind will revive spirits and give everyone the renewed energy to set up camp, get firewood, and prepare a more elaborate evening meal.

Desserts

There are many options available for desserts on travel days, including dried fruit, *s'mores*, instant cheesecakes, puddings, and even brownie mix. After having tried these and other desserts over the years, we typically bring just dried fruit and the makings of *s'mores* for desserts on the days we're traveling, because neither are hard to make or require dirtying more dishes.

Most members of our extended family enjoy choosing and preparing a good *s'more* stick, then impaling marshmallows and toasting them over the coals until they're golden brown. As everyone knows, if you place a

few small squares of chocolate bar on a graham cracker, then slide the toasted marshmallow on top and sandwich it with a second cracker, the heat of the marshmallow will begin to melt the chocolate and turn the creation into a delicious, gooey mess. The ingredients for *s'mores* are easy to pack and there is almost no clean-up involved!

79

On duff days we often take a different approach to desserts. Not only do we typically have more time and energy to make desserts on those days, we're also likely to have berries! Picking whatever berries are in season is always a popular activity. Wild strawberries ripen first, followed by raspberries and blueberries; sometimes all three are ripe simultaneously. When picking is good, four people can gather enough blueberries for both pancakes and a dessert in an hour. And fresh fruit can be transformed into sweet, hot compote in just a few minutes. Using the reflector over technique described on pages 59-60, we have succeeded in making everything from turnovers and open-faced tarts to fruit pies.

Dried fruit compote: We first encountered fruit compote on a cold winter night many years ago in a high class restaurant in New York. The initial surprise at being served "fruit soup" was soon replaced by the realization that it warmed us

1 C chopped fruit
water
1 t cinnamon
⅓ C sugar

wonderfully and also satisfied our sweet cravings. That very night we resolved to make fruit compotes while camping on cool nights.

Begin by simply placing dried mixed fruit (chopped) into a pot, cover it with water and boil it gently until the fruit softens. Add cinnamon and sugar, mix well and simmer the compote briefly. This is a great way to end an evening meal in May, early June, or September, when your compote-filled cup warms your cold hands, steams your face, and then delights your taste buds.

Fruit (berry) compote: Place fresh blueberries in a pot, add water, sugar, and cinnamon. Mix these ingredients well, then boil them briefly. Fresh fruit, especially blueberries, quickly wilt and lose water to the mixture. Once the berries

2 C fresh blueberries
water
½ C sugar
1-2 t cinnamon

are wilted and all the ingredients are hot and well-mixed, adjust the sweetness and cinnamon one final time and serve everyone a taste in a cup. Be prepared to make more.

1½ C flour
1-2 t baking powder
6 T lard or shortening
3-6 T water

Turnovers and open-faced fruit tarts: The same pastry and filling recipes can be used to make both turnovers and open-faced fruit tarts. The best pastry and pie-crust dough is made using lard; this dough is pliable and easy to work, and produces flaky, delicious, pastries and pies. Lard also stores reasonably well and can be carried in food packs in watertight plastic containers. If lard

Turnovers and open-faced tarts.

isn't a viable option, vegetable shortening and some brands of margarine also work well. The dough will be harder to work and the pastry less flaky, but the result will be still tasty. Unfortunately, both vegetable shortening and margarine can melt and convert to oil in warm weather and are less useful then. We've tried to make pastry and pie crust with oil alone and don't recommend it.

For turnovers, combine the flour and baking powder in a small pot and mix well. Now cut in the lard, vegetable shortening, or margarine until there are no balls larger than a small pea. Slowly add water and work it in with your hands. Stop adding water when the dough can be formed into a large ball that holds together well and seems pliable.

Rolling the dough for cutting and forming into turnovers and tarts is easy to do. Some old-timers (and young people fond of the old ways) like to use flat paddle blades or the smooth bottom of an overturned canoe as the rolling surface, but public health officials now universally reject that practice because it could introduce disease-causing microbes into the dough. We use our griddle, which provides a clean, broad surface. The underside of a pot lid can serve the same function.

For a rolling pin, try using a personal water bottle made of hard plastic. Simply place a ball of dough on the rolling surface and work the dough with the bottle until it has been flattened uniformly to about ¼ inch. Use the cap from a jar to cut the dough into 4-inch diameter circles and set them aside.

The filling of turnovers and tarts can be made easily with either dried or fresh fruit, but tarts require more fruit. If using dried fruit, place chopped dried fruit (raisins, cranberries, currants, and apricots all work well) into a small pot, cover the fruit with water and boil gently for ten minutes.

I C fruit	
¼ C sugar	
I t cinnamon	

When the dried fruit begins to soften, add the sugar and cinnamon and mix well. If possible use a fork or spoon to mash the fruit a bit. If using fresh blueberries, simply place the berries into a small pot, then add the sugar and cinnamon and mix well. Fresh berries do not need to be boiled but should be mashed a bit.

To construct the turnovers, place a small spoonful of filling onto one half of a pastry circle, then fold the other half up and over the filling. Wet and then pinch the edges of the turnover together to completely enclose and contain the filling. Be sure to poke a few holes in the upper surface of each turnover with the tines of a fork so they don't explode while baking.

To construct the tarts, fold the edges of a pastry circle inward to make a ridge that is about twice the depth of the remaining dough and which creates a cavity for the filling. Now simply spoon the filling into the cavity. Just before baking both the turnovers and tarts, we brush melted margarine, oil, milk, or soy milk on the upper surface of the dough (to help it brown) and sprinkle sugar on top.

The easiest way to bake the turnovers and tarts is to construct a reflector oven using heavy-duty aluminum foil. Simply fold the foil into a dome that is at least six inches high and large enough so that the griddle or frying pans that will serve as the baking sheet can slide smoothly under it into the make-shift oven. Wait until the coals are well-developed, then place the foil oven onto the grate above them. Wait a minute or two for the oven to heat up, then slide the turnovers or tarts in.

Both turnovers and tarts cook in about 15 minutes at 400 degrees, but many campfire reflector ovens are far hotter than that, so cooking times may be shorter. Maintaining a uniform temperature inside a reflector oven over an open fire is tricky, which makes it especially important to monitor the progress of the pastries as they bake. It may be necessary to add some small sticks to the fire from time to time, but don't add too many or you'll create an inferno inside the oven.

Blueberry pie: When on a canoe trip during blueberry season, most people pick blueberries for a snack or to add to pancakes, but relatively few groups take the time to make blueberry pies. Duff days are often great both for prolonged blueberry picking and for the preparation of a pie. Baking a pie with a reflector oven over a fire can be tricky because it's often difficult to maintain a consistent temperature under the reflector oven for an extended period, but we have learned some steps that make it easier to make a great pie over a cooking fire. For example, it's a good idea to cook the blueberries a bit before putting the pie together; this reduces the baking time of the pie.

4 C blueberries
½ C sugar
2 t cinnamon
4 T flour
2 C graham cr. crumbs
½ C powdered sugar
½ C margarine

Begin by adding fresh blueberries to a pot with a little water and then place the pot over the fire. Cook the blueberries until they soften, stirring frequently so they don't burn. After several minutes, remove the pot from the fire, add sugar, cinnamon, and flour, mix all ingredients well and then set aside while you make the crust.

Now crush graham crackers and place the crumbs into a small pot. Mix the crumbs with powdered sugar and melted butter or margarine.

Pat this mixture onto the bottom and sides of a frying pan.

When the crust is ready, pour the filling into the pan and then place the pie into a reflector oven made with heavy-duty aluminum foil. As with all baking done with reflector ovens, it's critical to control the fire during the cooking process. Pies are best baked over a good bed of coals with relatively little flame and smoke. Be sure to monitor the progress of the pie and remove it from the oven when the crust begins to brown (20 to 30 minutes).

We sometimes sprinkle a little brown sugar on the surface of the pie during the last few minutes of cooking.

9

Miscellaneous Tips

Cooking gear

It's a good idea to bring several bundles of "strike anywhere" matches in zip-lock bags or water-tight containers and place them here and there in several packs. (We often put the striker off the box into the bag as well.) Matches are very light so you might as well bring plenty. Starting a fire under adverse conditions can use up quite a few.

Those who travel light and like to "single-portage" might consider it a burdensome luxury, but a two-burner camp-stove can be a godsend, especially when conditions are rainy and the placement of the campground fire grate makes tarp-rigging in that location difficult or impossible. In most campsites there is some place where the arrangement of trees makes it possible to rig up a shelter from rain or high winds, thus keeping campers and equipment dry while also providing a more pleasant environment for cooking over the stove.

We usually bring a lightweight griddle on canoe trips. Many of the recipes in this book call for one, though with smaller groups a frying pan would suffice. We fold it into our tarp and pack it away in a Duluth pack.

Our cook kit contains three pots and two frying pans that form a compact nested unit. When packing we fill the smallest pot with convenient kitchen items ranging from Scrubbies to silverware and cups. Plates and silverware also fit inside. We place the packed cook kit into a stout canvas bag so the soot on the outside of the largest pot doesn't soil other things in the pack.

We rank our two plastic cutting boards among our most cherished cooking tools. These boards are easily washed and packed, and save "wear and tear" on both our plates and knives. Prior to the purchase of these boards we used aluminum plates for a cutting surface, resulting in dull knives and scratched plates (which are harder to clean). We usually pack one of the cutting boards in our cook kit for use in dinner preparation and fit the other in a box pack (described later in this chapter) near our lunch supplies.

Other handy items are a spatula, at least one long-handled wooden spoon, two small sheath knives, and a "Leatherman" multi-tool unit that we use for lifting pots off the fire, among other things. A thick glove or small oven mitt can also be useful.

We always pack biodegradable soap (e.g. "Campsuds") for washing dishes, at least one "scrubber" of some sort, and a sponge or wash cloth.

Cooking in the rain

Weather can be the glory or the bane of a canoe trip, and cooking in the rain presents special challenges. There are times when a group would just as soon give up the attempt, climb into their tents, and hope for better things to come. But with proper equipment and a little expertise, hot meals can be prepared under adverse conditions with relative ease.

The first step is to rig up a tarp above the fire-pit or stove. This is usually done by running a tight rope between two trees, draping the tarp over it, and fastening the corners to trees or stakes to keep it in place. It's important to keep the tarp well above the fire so it

isn't damaged by sparks or excessive heat, and also to fix the ends of the tarp as low to the ground as possible to prevent the wind from inflating it mercilessly like a sail. We usually bring a large tarp (20x30') under which campers, equipment, and firewood can all find a place to stay dry. I can recall rollicking card tournaments that took place under tarps during both torrential downpours and snowstorms.

Although we generally avoid cooking lunches during travel days, there are times when it makes good sense to do so. For example, severe storms can leave a group stranded for prolonged periods on a portage or at a campsite where they'll eventually get chilled, even with the best clothing and equipment. On one such occasion, we were able to fit our cook stove under a carefully overturned and propped aluminum canoe, and we boiled some water for instant soup and hot chocolate. Warm drinks had a dramatic effect on group morale and enabled us to travel on happily when the storm lifted.

Canoeing with kids

Introducing young people to the Northwoods carries special risks and rewards. I've traveled the border trail with children as young as six months, and several times have included two- and three-year-olds in the mix. Very young children require special care, but often have an energy and eye-opening enthusiasm for nature that's contagious.

Because children can be fussy about food, it's important to include some items you're sure that each child can and will eat; hungry kids often become unhappy kids and this can be problematic. Special monitoring will also be required to insure that such foodstuffs last the entire trip, keeping in mind that not only children but also adults can be tempted by honey-nut Cheerios, fruit leathers, and teething biscuits.

Small children often sit in the "duff compartment" of canoes, and they'll be happier there if they have activities or sturdy toys to play with. When our daughters were small they enjoyed portaging small backpacks that contained their raingear, a few books, a beanie baby, playing cards, and a packet of waterproof, permanent markers to convert white birch sticks into "birch people" dolls. Indeed, on those trips anyone tending a fire had to take extra care so as not to inadvertently immolate one of these dear birch people, each of whom had a name and a distinct personality. The same markers can also be used to draw and send secret messages on stray pieces of birchbark, providing many hours of fun on rainy days when a group is trapped under a tarp or in a tent.

All of the children we have traveled with in canoe county asked (at surprisingly early ages) to transition from carrying backpacks with toys on portages to carrying Duluth packs filled with gear. Fortunately, Duluth packs come in different sizes, and we were always able to find one suitable for a young camper to carry. These kids were empowered by taking part in our portaging chores. It was often the first step toward fuller participation in all aspects of life around the campsite.

Packing tips

In the course of our many forays through the Northwoods, my family and I have developed fairly sophisticated systems for organizing and packing our food. This enables us to provide a set of eating options to match our diverse tastes. We utilize some techniques that were common forty years ago but are now forgotten or ignored by most groups, though we also rely heavily on modern food storage equipment.

If you've read through the recipes in this book, you'll see that we often bring fragile and perishable foods on our trips. It isn't as hard as you might think to keep such things whole and fresh. We bring fresh eggs, tomatoes, and other perishables in cardboard boxes of various sizes for protection, making sure the boxes stay at the very top of the food pack. We pack foods that might leak—for example, plastic bottles of maple syrup—in plastic bags which then go into a suitable box. It's wise in some cases to provide extra cushioning. For example, we often surround fresh tomatoes with bags of marshmallows; this technique doesn't affect the mallows but can give us fresh tomatoes for lunch for up to a week!

When repacking the food packs in the morning, we insert a box into the top of one and fill it with all the fragile lunch items we'll need that day, including crackers and fresh vegetables, along with cheese and sausage, small bags of dried fruit, and gorp. We also place a clean cutting board, knife, cup, and spoon in this box along with instant hummus mix and a jar of peanut butter. We pack other lunch materials into a synthetic "dry bag" that can be easily identified—often by its unique size and color. We place this lunch bag immediately below the box pack that contains lunch material so we can reach it easily if we need it. When traveling, we often leave our canoes loaded and in the water, removing only the box pack and perhaps the lunch dry bag from the canoes; these items will contain all the food and gear needed for lunch. This organization saves both time and frustration every lunch break.

We use "dry bags" of various sizes and colors to organize our food for breakfasts and dinners in the same way. These bags, available at many sporting goods stores, are durable, difficult for small mammals to chew their way into, and water-tight. Most commercially available dry bags also have a handle of sorts which makes them easy to carry around in a campsite and to hang from trees.

Though fragile vegetables need the protection of boxes, you can place durable vegetables such as onions and garlic in plastic bags with the particular dinner they're meant to be a part of. It's important to make sure any carrots you bring are perfectly dry; otherwise, they may get moldy when sealed in a plastic bag. We usually put carrots into a box pack to make them accessible for lunches.

Fresh meat should only be packed frozen, wrapped in insulation and put inside a plastic bag and then placed in a box; this meat will thaw during the day and be ready to eat the first night of the trip. Meat with preservatives, such as some brands of summer sausage, are durable and do not need special treatment.

Cheeses coated with wax survive better in food packs than those that aren't.

Special dietary needs and issues

In any large group there are likely to be one or two individuals with special dietary issues. Our extended family can boast quite an array, from gluten-intolerant, wheat-intolerant, and lactose-intolerant individuals to those who are allergic to peanuts and vegetarian due to gout. Before planning a canoe trip menu, it's important to determine what the special needs of a group are going to be. Special dislikes and preferences ought also to be fully explored before shaping a menu. It's well worth the effort to hold a pre-trip planning session to hash out these issues.

Many such food issues are easy to address, and those who suffer from dietary challenges will be able to offer ideas. For example, people who are celiacs or otherwise intolerant of wheat can eat wheat- and gluten-free bread, crackers, and pasta that are easy to find in supermarkets. Similarly, it isn't hard to find products that lack milk if lactose-intolerant people are in the party, and to replace milk with soy milk in mixes and recipes. In such situations we bring well-marked bags of both dried milk and soy milk powder.

To accommodate vegetarians, we plan meals that allow some people to eat meat but do not require everyone to do so. For example, on "taco night" we make the quantity of taco meat that we think our meat-eaters will consume and prepare larger quantities of rice, refried beans, and toppings for everyone to eat. In fact, most of the dinner recipes in this book that include meat also could "stand alone" if prepared without the meat.

Gluten-free Granola

12 C rolled oats
3 C mixed nuts
½ C gluten free flour
1 C flax seed meal
2 T cinnamon
2 C flaked coconut
1 C sesame seeds
½ C honey
4 T molasses
1 C cooking oil
2 T vanilla
dash almond extract
2 t cinnamon
½ C water
2 C raisins

If some members of your group suffer from hypertension, seek out mixes with relatively low salt-content or make them yourself at home. Because diabetics need to control their sugar and carbohydrate intake, it's a good idea to bring more sausage, cheese, and both fresh and dried vegetables if diabetics are in the party.

Keeping food dry

The two things that present a significant risk to food preservation on any canoe trip are water and animals. If a bear gets at your food you've got a problem, and may have to abort the trip. By the same token, if your food packs get wet, your evening meal may not turn out very well. And if you dump in a rapids and your food pack never returns to the surface, it's probably time to head for home.

Fortunately, it's much easier to keep food safe from water damage now than it was forty years ago, when Duluth packs were made of untreated canvas. Modern Duluth packs are water resistant/repellent, and there are quite a few synthetic packs on the market.

Meanwhile, plastic bag technology has also improved dramatically during that time span. Quart- or gallon-sized bags that can be sealed keep food dry and safe more reliably than cling-wrap or twist-ties ever did. We place all non-perishable foods for a given meal in a "dry bag" with a water-tight seal, having purchased bags of different sizes and colors to make it easier to pick out which meal is which. And we line our Duluth packs with a heavy-duty pack liner manufactured for that purpose. These liners aren't water tight at the top but they protect things from the rain, snow, and the water that tends to slosh back and forth at the bottom of a canoe.

These cheerful "dry-bags" have been hung where they'll challenge the ingenuity of any hungry bear.

Keeping food safe from animals

Bears are not encountered very often in the border country, but they're everywhere, and are adept at stealing or damaging the food of canoeists. They're most likely to take an interest in your food at night or when you're away from the site. The best way to foil bears, therefore, is to avoid leaving food unattended in camp. We often load food packs into canoes and carry it with us when we head out for a day of fishing or on an evening paddle.

Simply hanging a food pack on a branch or a piece of rope at night only makes it easier for a bear to find it, unless the lowest part of a food pack is at least eight feet above the ground; the pack should also be at least four feet *below* the branch that supports it and at least six feet laterally from nearby trunks. Many canoeists underestimate the ability of bears to reach packs from the ground or to jump onto them from above or from nearby trees.

Some campsites have trees with branches suitable for keeping food packs effectively out of the reach of bears, but many do not. One good method is to run a rope between two trees and tie the food packs to it, then raise them high overhead by pulling the rope taut.

To get the rope over a high branch, tie a rock to one end and then throw the rock (and rope) over the limb. But be forewarned, the rock will probably sail off into the woods whether the rope reaches the branch or not. It's much easier to place a rock into a used, mesh onion sack and then tie the bag securely to the end of the rope.

A few members of our group are great tree climbers and quickly scale tree trunks to place the hanging ropes wherever we need them.

When hanging food packs is not a viable option, it's a good idea to put the food packs under an overturned canoe. We often plug the openings at the ends of the canoe with logs and place empty pots and plates on top of it for a "bear-scare." If the bear disturbs the canoe the pots and pans will fall and clatter, at which point we emerge from our tents as quickly as possible and make sufficient noise to drive the bear away.

The bears found in the Quetico and BWCAW are black bears, and are more of a nuisance than a danger to campers. They're strong and well-armed, however, and it's important to always leave them an avenue of escape when driving them from camp. If you surround one then someone may be run over and hurt when the bear escapes.

Gray jays aren't shy, and they're curious about your food.

A bear that successfully grabs a food pack will be reluctant to give it back, and attempts to wrestle the pack away would be foolhardy, to say the least. Female bears that bring cubs into camp can be especially dangerous. These females will not leave their babies, and if the cubs are frightened and climb a tree, then you're likely to have visitors for a prolonged period. When this occurs the best solution may be to quickly move camp.

Although a bear can destroy most of a group's food during a single visit, this is a rare occurrence in the border country. When you pick up your permit at the forest service office, the ranger will be able to tell you specific lakes or portages where bear encounters have been reported recently. The animals that present problems most frequently in the woods aren't bears but small mammals such as red squirrels, chipmunks, mice, and red-backed voles. Most campsites are within the home range of at least one pair of red squirrels, and they'll forage on spilled food and also invade food packs. They'll even chew into heavy-duty plastic bags of food if given enough time.

Squirrels and chipmunks are active only during daylight and can be foiled by guarding food packs and taking them with you when you leave the campsite unattended. Mice and voles are nocturnal and can be shockingly abundant at some campsites. Both mice and voles invade food packs, including packs hung from trees; they gain access to the packs by climbing down the ropes that suspend the packs. These small mammals are capable of chewing through thick "dry bags," but this has only happened rarely.

Once, years ago, I was camped near Lower Basswood Falls early in the fall with a group of college students. Our campsite clearly had been used heavily throughout the summer, but it was clean of trash and there was no evidence of recent bear activity. We found ample supplies of firewood nearby, and following a nice dinner most of us gathered around the campfire. We had a wonderful time chatting around the fire, but eventually decided to let it die down and turn our attention to the stars and the sounds of the night.

Some of us had just turned our backs to the fire, the better to view the stars over the lake, when one student exclaimed, "I see eyes, more eyes. My God they're everywhere!" We switched on our headlamps and realized we were surrounded by scores of voles and mice that were waiting patiently for us to go to sleep so they could ransack our camp.

Student reaction to this abundance of small mammals was mixed. Several became almost unhinged and immediately retreated to their tents and sleeping bags, while one student tried to drive the "furry hoards" off the site with a barrage of well-aimed rocks. Needless to say, these efforts were futile, though they provided the rest of us with some unusual entertainment.

The few remaining students helped me wrap our food packs in an old tarp and stash them under the canoes. During the night, small mammals did penetrate the packs in one or two places but caused little damage.

Two students reported the next day that they had had nightmares about being attacked by mice.

Keeping Fish

Many canoeists incorporate fresh fish into their diets at least a few times during trips into the Quetico and BWCAW. Typically fisherfolks place the fish they catch onto stringers to keep them alive and fresh until it's time to eat. Some construct fish weirs of rocks near shore to use as holding tanks. When left unattended, fish on stringers and in holding tanks may attract the attention of snapping turtles or river otters. Snapping turtles are very common throughout Ontario and Minnesota, and often visit campsites in search of food. A single large snapping turtle can eat most of a large walleye or bass in a relatively short period. Snappers are so abundant that we do not leave fish unattended for very long,

especially overnight. Large, wire-mesh baskets protect fish from snappers but are bulky and a nuisance to carry over portages; you rarely see such baskets used more than one portage from entry points. River otters aren't as abundant as snapping turtles but often travel in family groups and can quickly decimate fish kept on stringers or in a holding

Pine martens roam the Northwoods— though they're seldom spotted.

tank. We once lost five "keeper" pike to a family of otters in the brief time it took us to gather firewood for dinner.

Many other animals commonly visit campsites but do not represent serious threats to food supplies or people. Gray jays, also known as Canada jays, whisky-jacks or camp robbers, often visit campsites during mealtimes and may take hand-outs or even steal food from hot griddles, but they eat very little and are harmless. Other birds, including roughed grouse and various woodpeckers (e.g. yellow-bellied sapsuckers) may be commonly sighted at campsites but simply live at those sites and will not eat your food. Lucky campers might also see a moose, fisher, pine marten, mink, or even a wolf near camp, but these wonderful creatures aren't interested much in your food.

Night Sounds

One of the most pleasant moments in any canoe trip is when you're lying comfortably in the tent listening to the sounds of the night. Many campers recognize the hooting "Who cooks for yooooou?" call of the barred owl, and the hooting of the great gray owl can also be heard in some northern forests. During a recent September trip, we realized that the frequent hissing noises we were hearing during the night were made by migrating saw-whet owls; these tiny owls were quite tame and allowed us to approach to within a few feet of them.

To hear the nocturnal call of the whip-poor-will in or near moist woodlands can be a thrill—though the song is so loud and persistent that we're likely to be relieved when it finally stops. The call of the common loon is more varied and haunting—so much so that for many it epitomizes the Northwoods experience. The white-throated sparrow occasionally produces its haunting, somewhat deranged "Sam Peabody" call during otherwise quiet nights. It's also common during spring and fall migrations to hear the honking of Canada geese as they fly overhead during the night.

As for amphibians, it isn't unusual during spring and early summer to hear the mating songs of spring peepers, wood frogs, chorus frogs, gray treefrogs, mink frogs, northern leopard frogs, green frogs, and American toads in canoe country, though few canoeists know which is which.

Insects also contribute to this gentle evening cacophony. There are times when the sound of mosquitoes in flight can be almost deafening, like the drone of a not-too-distant freeway. Another common insect noise is the chewing of wood-boring beetles known as longhorn or sawyer beetles. These beetles have large mandibles and are surprisingly loud as they work their way through a piece of wood.

Mammals also contribute to the nocturnal orchestra from time to time. You might hear the howl of a wolf or a pack of wolves, though that critter can also make other vocalizations. During a recent September I camped on a small, marshy campsite on Jackfish Bay of

A not-uncommon sight in the border country.

Basswood Lake with a group of college students. We had arrived at that site late in the day and were cooking dinner in the dark when a pack of wolves passed nearby and stopped to interact with one another. They didn't howl in the classic manner but made a clamor of barks, growls, yips and shrieks; a student later described it as the "caterwauling of banshees." Indeed, my students weren't entirely convinced that wolves had made these noises until later in the night when we heard wonderful long howling choruses from these and other, more distant wolves.

Other common mammal-made night sounds include the tail-slapping of beavers on the surface of lakes, the alarm snorts of white-tailed deer, and the loud footfalls of both deer and moose. Many inexperienced canoeists mistake both the snorting of deer and their noisy movement in the forest for more ominous animals, especially bears. In fact, bears usually come into camp silently; they may snuffle softly and sometimes make a wheezing exhalation through their nose that is unmistakable, but adults do not often vocalize.

Many other animals often enter and exit campsites quietly, including mink, pine martens, and fishers. Smaller mammals such as mice and voles often are noisy in camp during the night, scurrying near, under, and on the tents, bumping into tent ropes, and rustling under the tarp and in packs. Very early in the morning red squirrels can make quite a racket with their vocalizations and scampering about the campsite.

For Further Reading

Routes

For further information on canoe trip routes, the two volumes of *Boundary Waters Canoe Area* by Robert Beymer provide comprehensive information about the length and difficulty of a large number of popular routes in the BWCAW. This reference guide also gives you some idea of the relative popularity of a given entry point or chain of lakes and the likely water level at different times of year, all of which can be valuable when deciding where to put in and which route to take.

We have also used information in *Magic on the Rocks: canoe country pictographs*, by Michael Furtman, to develop specialized routes that allowed us to view several pictograph sites on a single trip. Furtman describes the location and paintings found at most of the pictograph sites in both the Quetico and the BWCAW.

The *Boundary Waters Journal* is a quarterly publication that includes many articles on canoe trip routes, camping equipment and techniques, cooking and menus, fishing, and natural history. The *BWJ* website (*www.boundarywatersjournal.com*) includes a useful trip-planning service for subscribers.

Once you've arived in the Northwoods, outfitters in both Minnesota and Ontario also can be wonderful sources of supplemental information about canoe trip routes, equipment, menus, and fishing. Local bait shops are usually happy to share up-to-date information about fishing holes, lures, and equipment.

Natural history

Many field guides are availiable to help you identify and learn more about the organisms and communities of the boundary waters area. I am most familiar with and prefer the Peterson series, especially the volumes on eastern birds, butterflies, mammals, animal tracks, ferns, trees and shrubs, reptiles and amphibians, wildflowers, insects, and beetles. The Sibley and Audubon guides also have their devotees.

Anyone wishing to develop a deeper understanding of the interrelationships of various Northwoods flora and fauna might find the *Sierra Club Naturalist's Guide to the North Woods* useful, though it's long out of print. *The Field Guide to Wildlife Habitats of the Eastern United States* might also come in handy, though its scope extends far beyond the boreal forest environment.

Visitors to Quetico Provincial Park may have the opportunity, when checking into the park, to purchase booklets on the butterflies, mammals, and reptiles of the park, and books such as *Quetico Fishes* by E. J. Crossman, and *Plants of Quetico and the Ontario Shield* by Shan Walshe.

Visitors to the BWCAW may be interested in a U.S. Forest Service publication on the Birds of the Superior National Forest, or in *The Mammals of Minnesota* by Evan B. Hazard, *The Ferns of Minnesota* by RollaTryon, or *The Boundary Waters Wilderness Ecosystem* by Miron (Bud) Heinselman. Heinselman spent many years studying fire scars to document and map the fire history of the region. He here presents the fruits of his research and explains the role of forest fire in shaping forest communities.

In *The Forest for the Trees: how humans shaped the north woods*, Jeff Forrester offers a brief but readable look at the changing ecosystem of the Northwoods extending from aboriginal times through the logging era and the long legal battle to preserve the region's recreational resources, and on to the recent blow-down and the fires of the twenty-first century.

History and Literature

The classic works of Grace Lee Nute, *The Voyaguers* and *Rainy River Country*, still make a good introduction to the fur trade era in the border country. A far more graphic acount of the same period is *The Falcon: a Narrative of the Captivity and Adventures of John Tanner.* Tanner was captured in 1789 and spent three decades living among the Ojibwe in the Northwoods. An abridged version of his account of the experience, originally published in 1830, was reprinted in 1994.

Nowadays Northwoods literature tends far more often to the meditative vein of works such as Sigurd Olson's *Listening Point*, Louise Erdrich's *Islands and Books in Ojbwe Country*, and *Boundary Waters: The Grace of the Wild*, by Paul Gruchow. The anthology *North Writers: A Strong Woods Collection*, edited by John Hendricksson, would be a good place to begin an exploration of writers seeking to capture the elusive magic of the border region.

Recipe Index